MASTERPIECE

OF

THE MASTER

BY SHARLEY ALLISON

Wordclay
1663 Liberty Drive, Suite 200
Bloomington, IN 47403
www.wordclay.com

First published by Wordclay on 5/30/2009.
ISBN: 978-1-6048-1770-6 (sc)

Printed in the United States of America.

This book is printed on acid-free paper.

Note from the author
Please read first

It is the duty of authors of works such as these to give credit to all who played a part in its composure. This book, presented as a fictional allegory designed to portray both God's absolute love for mankind and His extreme abhorrence of sin, includes many items given to me through the prophetic utterance. Therefore the words belong to God. The story is fictional, serving the purpose of allowing each person to sort through its contents and discover what God is speaking individually. It is by no means intended to establish any new doctrine but rather to present a side of God that we often overlook. Thus the burden of responsibility concerning how to interpret these contents rests solely upon the reader. As God deals with all on a very personal level, the story is not intended to explain His entire workings with everyone. Instead, it provides a picture of His desire to rid us each of the disease of sin. The intensity of His love for us is matched only by His extreme hatred for sin and its destructive power.

This allegory is the tale of one young girl's journey to discover who Jesus is and what He desires for His people. In many ways Kara, the main character, is representative of the Church, the bride of Christ. Her name means pure, and her plight is a picture of the collective journey of believers, our battle against willful sin, and the striving of Jesus' Body to enter into completion in Him. One is best served to understand that though the pages seem harsh on the surface, God's desire is to change our hearts rather than to punish. Unfortunately, due to the deceitfulness of sin and the hardness of our hearts, these two concepts seem to be inseparably intertwined; for God hates sin and its destructiveness in our lives to such a degree that He will go to great lengths to remove it from us. He is not cruel as some might take these word pictures to represent; rather He is more interested in the eternal state of our hearts than in the temporal comforts of the flesh, though it truly pains Him to bring us to the necessary repentance. He loves us enough to take us through the process required to cleanse us of our desire to cling to our unrighteousness, though we often do not appreciate His painstaking labor on our behalf. Though He desires that we each readily and completely accept His work on the cross for us, we often resist, requiring that our hearts be brought to full repentance. Thus, though not necessarily in such a literal fashion as depicted in Kara's story, we suffer much. Yet even in this there is great reward, if we will simply embrace His work in us, accepting as Paul states that "… the sufferings of this present time are not worthy to be compared with the glory which shall be revealed in us." (Romans 8:18b KJV).

Though not exhaustive in nature, included in these pages are answers to many basic questions and the responses to numerous objections to the gospel of Jesus Christ. The goal of this work is to create an intense hunger for His presence, coupled with a willingness to embrace His necessary discipline to obtain the prize of intimate relationship with Him. I pray that God will speak to each reader as He desires. Please allow Him to plant the things in your heart which He desires to show you, and if anything seems contrary to scripture, assign it to that portion of your mind that seeks God for the truth of the matter.

Chapter 1

Sergeant Merdail wanted nothing more than to cover his ears and close his eyes as the blaring of horns and sirens, mixed with the odor of blood, dirt, and burnt rubber, filled the night about him. The screams of the teens lying on the road about his feet were almost more than he could bear. Where were the parents, and why had these kids been out at such a late hour? The smell of alcohol was overpowering, with broken beer bottles strewn everywhere, and these children were dying before his eyes. Usually able to maintain the necessary cold professionalism in these situations, his thirty years of repeated death and sorrow were ganging up on him now. Medical personnel were on the scene, and the sight was hitting too close to home, his own two teens in sharp focus in his mind. He knew it would be a miracle if any of these children lived, their bodies so mangled on the road and their voices crying out to a God that they obviously did not know up to this time.

Off to the side was the body of a young girl, barely breathing and silent before him. Her face seemed to fairly shine, and he marveled as amidst the darkness and bloody mess, he could still observe that she was much different than the other five. She looked like a little broken porcelain doll, he thought, almost like an angel, though the glass from the windshield that had cut her had practically shredded her body. Trying desperately to hide his tears as the paramedics came over to the pile of blood and flesh that lay in his path with barely a breath of life still in it, he walked over to the side of the road and threw up.

The task of paper work and attempts at identification were overwhelming. How could he possibly speak to these parents? His compassion was clouded by an inward rage that these children had been able to escape the notice of their parents to leave home after curfew, and that someone had assisted them in purchasing so much alcohol. He recognized one of the boys, Daniel, whose father was a known felon, but the rest of these kids were strangers to him.

"Joe," sounded a voice from behind him. It was Larry, his partner. He briefly turned his head to acknowledge the address, still desiring to hide his own emotions. "There is no identification on most of these kids. The driver has a suspended license, so we can call his parents. It doesn't look like he made it. He was just seventeen. This is going to be a long night."

"I recognize this boy over here. His dad is serving time for raping a teen on her way home from the high school. He was up for several other charges as well, but the evidence on those fell through. Guess I will have to call the boy's mother. He doesn't look to make it either. I'll be surprised if any of these kids survive the night." Sergeant Merdail managed to shove his emotions into the very last storage place left within his soul, absorbing the shock of the task at hand. There would be a reckoning later, as he would have to make space for the next disaster, but for this moment, his mechanical movements overtook his emotions. This was the only way he could successfully perform his job as was expected of him. "Guess I had better start making calls," he mumbled. There were so many loose ends, so many things he did not know, and many of the pieces would take much longer to put together than he could comprehend. But then, that is because he did not know the rest of the story.

．．．

Fifteen-year-old Kara looked out the window, contemplating the boredom of the day. Even the lush green grass and a row of yellow tulips, the sounds of birds chattering, and the tree branches moving in the faint breeze were nothing more than a mild annoyance. Summers always seemed such an eternity, though she was elated to be out of school. But mid July brought scorching heat, and she held no hope of a friend to talk with during her suffering. Her closest friend, Susanna, was on a family vacation in Kentucky, where she would remain until the new school year. Daniel had broken up with Kara a week ago when she refused to have sex with him, a fact she was not about to discuss this with her mother. "She'd probably just say I told you so," she fumed, tossing her long brown hair from her face.

"Breakfast is ready," she heard from downstairs. Why did they even bother? She might as well pretend to sleep till noon. Kara crawled back under the covers, taking a brief glance at the clothes strewn throughout the small room, but she was interrupted by a knock at the door. It was Mom. "Kara, you can't mope around all day. We need help getting everything ready. Grandma is coming this afternoon. Please come down and eat."

What did she mean, mope? How did she know anyway? Kara hadn't even told her about Daniel. She sure wasn't going to let on that Mom had touched a nerve. At least with Grandma visiting, maybe everyone would be too busy with her to bother Kara.

"What? I am still in bed! Isn't that what summer's are for?" She threw off the covers, tossed her pajamas on the floor, and pulled her shortest white shirt and blue shorts out of her drawer. Pulling them on and straightening her hair, Kara took a bit of pleasure in the notion that these clothes would annoy her mother. She stormed downstairs, slamming her bedroom door behind her.

The kitchen was bright and cheery with the smell of fresh coffee, fried bacon, pancakes, and hot maple syrup. Mom had put new cut tulips on the table, and Dad was drinking his coffee. He looked especially happy today, as he always did when he was expecting a visit from Grandma. Kara thought Grandma must be Dad's favorite person in the world, next to her at least.

At the table, Dad piped up with, "Good morning, Angel!" Angel? If he only knew what she was thinking! These guys really were clueless. Kara merely mumbled a brief hello and ate a few bites of bacon. "We need for you to clean the kitchen when you're done," he continued. "Isn't it going to be fun to see Grandma again?"

"Whatever," muttered Kara, drinking a tall glass of orange juice. "Can't we ever have anything besides burnt pancakes and bacon for breakfast? And who are we trying to impress with the flowers? Grandma isn't even here yet!"

"Guess someone woke up on the wrong side of the bed," continued Dad. "Might be a good time to pray and get the day started right." Kara ignored the remark and continued eating. They really did not know a thing about teens, and maybe not about anything else for that matter. Sure, God was real and all, but did they have to talk about Him all the time? What a waste of a perfectly miserable day!

If only there was someone to talk to, someone younger than thirty-five. Kara had always wanted a brother, and this was the perfect time to notice that he was not there. Even a sister would be better than nothing at this point, but she knew that wasn't going to happen. Mom couldn't have any more babies since she had so much trouble delivering Kara. They had done an emergency hysterectomy when they couldn't stop the bleeding. Sometimes Kara felt guilty that Mom had to give up her dream of having more children. It seemed like it was somehow her fault even though no one had ever suggested the idea.

But not today. Today she was just mad at the world and figured they all deserved any misery they got. She wasn't even sure why she was so angry, but Kara was vaguely disappointed that Mom hadn't said anything else to her. She had a list of retorts just on the tip of her tongue with no where to use them.

Kara finished her breakfast and began cleaning the kitchen. She found special pleasure in banging the cupboards as she put things away in the tiny kitchen, and her effort to clean the kitchen was hasty at best. She knew no one would dare to ask her to do anything else. When she finished, she stomped back up to her room and slammed the door.

Savannah choked back the tears as her daughter left the room. She did not know how to reach Kara anymore. She had prayed and prayed, but things just seemed to get worse. If she could only get Kara to talk with her, or even to listen, maybe it could be different. Though she remembered her own rough teen years, Savannah was sure it could be better for her own daughter. She had so many personal regrets, and though she had worked on receiving forgiveness, some things just continued to haunt her. How could she ever explain things to Kara? And if Kara knew her mother's background, would it make her hate her more?

Savannah's heart ached for her daughter, and her soul hemorrhaged for the son she had given up when she was pregnant at sixteen. She had no idea where he was or even if he was still alive. And though David, her husband, knew about the boy, even he did not know about the abortion her mother forced her to have at twelve. They said it was a girl. If only she could have somehow kept the baby, maybe she could feel better. Though she was raped by her uncle, she felt that it was partly her own fault. That's what her mother told her anyway. It was her fault for wearing a shirt that was a little too tight. She had to have an abortion so that her uncle wouldn't be sent to jail. Savannah never knew her own father, and when her mother died of a drug overdose on her seventeenth birthday, Savannah hid in a deserted house to stay away from her new guardian, her uncle. She survived from the food in the trash of a wealthy neighbor and by begging for food on the street. Rescued by a Christian family at eighteen, Savannah found Jesus. There she was taught how to cook, clean, and be a part of a family, and they cared for her until she could get a job. Though Savannah told herself that she had forgiven her mother and uncle, the wounds within continued to ooze with the infection of bitterness and agony.

Savannah met David and was married at twenty. Though she told David much of her background, she could not even bear to form the words to tell him about the abortion or the rape. That was just too much. His life had always been so perfect. Raised in a Christian home with two parents, his father died only a year ago, and his mother was still living. He could not possibly understand. She did not experiment with drugs the way her mother had, and unlike her mother, she had experienced sex with only two men, her uncle and the father of her son. Yet her life had been a living hell. Savannah spent her childhood hours hiding under beds and in closets for fear of the attention of the numerous men her mother brought into their lives. Since many of the men only stayed the night and her mother was high on drugs, most people did not even notice Savannah existed. She often stored bits of food and a cup of water in those places in case the men stayed too long, but it was especially difficult to sneak out when no one was looking to use the bathroom. This task was an exceptionally hard since they slept in so many places that Savannah had to remember where the bathroom was. But even the most ingenious child could not always avoid the uncle who was frequently with them. She still remembered his stale breath, the smell of alcohol and tobacco, and his sweaty hands when he touched her. She could feel the sting of his hand across her face as if it were yesterday as he slapped her for crying out as he put his body over hers. Though the loud music covered her cries, he did not allow her the luxury of expression. She shuddered as she remember the tearing of her skin and how he made her clean up her own blood, growling that she had better not tell anyone or he would make things much worse.

How could she relate to her own daughter? In some ways Savannah was even a bit jealous of what she viewed as the perfect life Kara had led, though she always wanted the best for her daughter. She just could not fathom why Kara was so angry and miserable. She also felt an extra pang of guilt every time Kara complained about not having any siblings. Savannah was aware that Daniel had broken up with Kara but could not understand what she saw in the boy anyway. It was obvious what he was after and that he did not care about her as a person at all. He was not even that attractive in Savannah's opinion.

Finishing up the house work and starting a pot of stew for lunch, Savannah waited for her mother-in-law to arrive. Though they were not close, as Grandma had always seemed disapproving of Savannah, she was the nearest thing to a mother the wounded girl possessed. Savannah craved that acceptance and tried very hard to please her. When Grandma was coming, the house had to be just right and in order, everything in its place. Savannah had to prove that she was a good wife to this woman's son.

....

David waited on the corner for the bus that would bring his mother to visit. He loved her visits, as they had always been quite close. He felt a bit guilty about the constant little jabs his mother sent Savannah's way during these times, but after all, what could you expect? An ex-street girl was not her idea of a good match for her son. Though he knew about Savannah's past when they were married, even he had moments of reservation thinking about the sordid details. He wondered how many men she had actually been with, though when tested at his request before their marriage, she came up clean of all sexually transmitted diseases. He had only been with three women intimately before her, and being a man, he felt that was pretty good. He knew they were both forgiven for the past, but thinking on these things gave him a feeling of mistrust towards his wife. What if she decided to go back to that old life? At least he was sure Kara had been protected from knowing her mother's former existence. All she knew was that Savannah's parents died before she was born and that there were no close relatives on that side of the family. It was mostly true anyway, as Savannah's mother had no idea who her baby's father was, and now her mother was dead. If Savannah ever did go that way, he would be sure Kara was kept away from her. Of course that would be easy with Kara's present contempt for her mom. He felt a strange comfort in that knowledge.

David brushed the ideas aside, feeling a twinge of discomfort at his thoughts, and told himself he was glad he had rescued his wife from her old life. He was glad God used him that way. He loved Savannah and Kara very much, and Savannah had proved to be a wonderful wife and a devoted mother. Mother and daughter looked so much alike with their long, wavy brown hair, pale skin, and short thin stature. And they both had that enticing smile and big brown eyes that could melt any angry heart. Seeing his own mother just seemed to bring back old dialogues, the things his mother had spoken about Savannah over the years. He often wished he had not told his mother so much about Savannah's past life, but the couple had been so excited about her transformation that they freely shared her testimony with nearly everyone.

The bus delivered Grandma as promised, and mother and son exchanged warm hugs. Grandma smelled of sweet perfume as she bent her slightly heavy five foot ten inch frame to climb into the car. Tossing back her gray head in a chuckle, she quipped, "What's for lunch? Hobo stew?" David laughed uneasily as he closed the door. It was just another joke at Savannah's expense.

....

Grandma's visit was uneventful, with Mom only leaving the room abruptly once. Overall Kara felt it went fairly well. She never understood why every little thing Grandma said seemed to bother Mom. What was it this time? Oh, yeah. It was something about how wonderful the mud pie was. It almost looked like Mom started to cry. What was the big deal? It was just a funny way of referring to the chocolate pudding pie at lunch. She would never understand grown-ups.

Up in her room, Kara pulled out her paint supplies. Looking at the bright colors, she was a little sorry she had been so testy with Mom this morning, but she certainly wasn't going to tell anyone. After all, Mom knew teens get cranky sometimes. She wouldn't take it that personally. Kara's art always cheered her up. She loved the intense oranges, reds, greens; well, she loved all shades. Kara actually enjoyed the faint smell of paint, because to her, each scent was a color, a form of self expression not attainable in any other way. She was determined to become an accomplished artist. Kara would display and sell her paintings, and one day, she would create the greatest masterpiece of all, the sum of all she ever felt and saw in her life. She would somehow paint Daniel out of her picture, excluding whatever colors reminded her of him, as he was deemed unworthy of that kind of attention. She imagined standing before crowds, presenting her wonderful works while others looked on, awed by what they saw.

Turning on the radio, she fumbled through the dials. Aware that her choice of music was less than pleasing to her parents, Kara turned up the music anyway. Ignoring a twinge of discomfort with the lyrics, she settled into a beat and sound that she enjoyed. Kara hesitated briefly when she heard the echo of a telephone ringing throughout the house, hoping someone else would answer it. Since she had insisted on having a phone in her room, her parents expected her to pick it up it on occasion. It looked like this was one of those times. She turned down the music slightly, and after the third ring, she grabbed the handset, annoyed. "Hello?"

The low voice on the other end was a boy. "Yeah, I'd like to talk with Savannah please," he retorted.

Not willing to go downstairs to get her mother, Kara replied that Savannah was not available. She asked if she could take a message.

"Yeah, well tell her that her son called. Tell her it is Jeremy."

"You have the wrong number," Kara grumbled, and she hung up.

When the phone rang again, Kara was exasperated. Still no one downstairs answered. "Hello," she repeated.

"Hey listen! Don't hang up. This is where Savannah McNeill lives, isn't it?" started the irritated voice.

Kara recognized the title as her mother's maiden name. "Yeah, but her name is Savannah Tells, and she doesn't have a son," she replied. "I think I would know. I've lived with her all my life. I'm her daughter!"

This time the voice sounded really angry. "Just tell her the son she doesn't have, the one she gave away nineteen years ago, is on the phone and wants to know why she was too ashamed of me to tell you I exist! And why she hasn't even tried to find out if I am even dead or alive! Tell her that!"

Kara nearly dropped the phone. Her whole heart felt numb. Her head was spinning. As she descended the stairs, each step seemed to taunt her. "You have a brother, and he hates you. You have a brother who was never allowed to look out for you. Your mother gave him away and never even told you. She just pretended to be sorry you were alone…"

At the bottom of the steps, she practically threw the phone at her mother and ran up the stairs. She flung herself on the bed, too overcome with a world of emotions to even cry. The beat of the music on the radio, which she had turned back up, seemed to intensify her anger. What a liar! What an evil woman to not even care about her own son. Maybe she only kept Kara because of Dad. Maybe she really didn't want her either. Kara could not sit, and she could not stand. She was completely paralyzed in a torrent of emotions that she did not understand.

Someone was at her door. Why had she not locked it? Within seconds, Dad entered the room. Turning down the music again and lightly touching her shoulder, he began to speak softly. "It was before I knew her. She was only sixteen. It was before she knew Jesus."

Kara jerked away, angrier that ever. "You knew? You both lied! Don't touch me! I hate her! I hate you both! You stole my brother! Why not give me away too?"

Stunned by the torrent of angry words, David walked helplessly from the room. He knew he had taught Kara that to hide the truth was a lie, but somehow this was different. David was not used to being on the other side of Kara's wrath. She had always been a Daddy's girl. He also knew that it was his decision to hide the truth from Kara.

Kara mustered all her strength to get to the door and lock it. She turned her music up louder than ever. What hypocrites! They had told her that she should not have sex until she was married, and now she had discovered that her mother had a son! She had a baby at sixteen years old! Her mom sure didn't wait! And why wasn't she even told she had a brother? Somehow she thought she had always sensed it; she had always missed him. It was just too much to process. The cocktail of rage, hurt, rejection, fear, and longing could not be swallowed at a single gulp, and Kara was choking on it.

Kara tried to pick up her paintbrush to place one huge angry color over her entire piece, but her arm would not move. Perhaps they had stolen her art as well. They had taken everything else. She was furious at God. Why hadn't He made them keep Jeremy? Why did He let them keep their secret so long? Maybe He was showing them up now! Surely they both deserved to go to Hell! Kara was too angry to even shudder at the thought.

Mom and Dad were arguing downstairs. "I told you we needed to tell her about him!" cried Mom. "This is not how I wanted Kara to find out she had a brother! I thought we were in this together!" she wailed. "He is coming tomorrow to see me, and he wants to meet Kara."

"Tell him to stay away!" yelled Dad. "He's caused enough trouble already! I do not want him anywhere near her!"

In a deep defiant voice quite uncharacteristic of Savannah came the words, "No! I want to see my son! And if Kara wants to meet her brother, she is going to see him! They have been kept apart long enough!"

"Yeah, well he's probably a sexual pervert like the rest of your family!" came the scathing reply. "Do you even know who his father is?" He regretted the words as soon as they escaped his lips, but he was not willing to take them back.

The words cut deep into her being, but Savannah merely walked into the bedroom and closed the door. For a split second, Kara felt sorry for her mother, but the sensation was quickly swallowed up in the anger and heat of the moment. "I will see my brother!" she screamed down the stairs, "and nobody is going to stop me!"

....

Kara tried to sleep, but her rest was fitful. She thrashed in her bed, thoughts racing faster than she could process them. She had never had trouble sleeping before, never even had a bad dream that she could remember, but this was different. Overcome with exhaustion, she slipped from consciousness.

Kara's slumber was filled with terror. She dreamed she was a little girl, playing with a Barbie doll. It was old, with a dirty pink dress and scraggly long brown hair. A tall man with dark hair walked up, hovering over her. He smelled awful, like sweat and dirt, and a mixture of other odors she could not even recognize. She had never seen the man before, but somehow Kara was sure she knew him. She jumped up in the dream and ran away, the man yelling after her. The louder he called the harder she ran. Terrified, she woke up. Her sheet had slipped over her face due to her thrashing movements, and for a moment she felt unable to breath, struggling to remove them from her face.

What was that? Perhaps she was just too upset before she went to sleep. Kara sat up in bed, her hair sticking to her cheeks and sweat running down her face, petrified to go back to sleep again. Scarcely able to catch her breath, Kara was afraid to make a move. She sat frozen in the same position for what seemed to be forever. There was a bit of comfort in the realization that at least she would meet her brother today. But what if he didn't like her? What was he like? He sounded so angry on the phone. Maybe he was mad that Mom had kept her and not him. What would Kara say to him? A rush of fear again filled the space about her.

Light slowly entered the room as the sun peaked in the window. What would she do till he came? She was too enraged to go downstairs with Mom and Dad. Maybe she would clean her room, since her brother might come up stairs. Kara quickly checked her door to be sure it was locked and began the task at hand. In the same way her room was strewn with dirty clothes and an unkempt bed, Kara knew she had been sloppy about talking with God each morning lately, so she quickly mumbled a prayer. "God help Jeremy to like me, and help me to somehow be able to talk to Mom and Dad again ….. since I have to live with them anyway," she muttered.

No one called up the stairs for breakfast. There were no familiar smells, no pleasant conversation. It was completely still in the house, except for the faint sounds of water running. Sneaking downstairs, Kara peeked around the corner into the kitchen. On the table sat a box of cereal, one lonely bowl, a spoon, and an empty cup. Mom was at the sink washing dishes, and Dad was no where in sight. Still angry but hungry for breakfast, Kara sat on a wooden chair at the table, and as Mom turned to bring milk for the cereal, there was no doubt in Kara's mind that her mother had been crying. Her long brown, wavy hair, freshly brushed, glistened in the light coming through the window, but the dark circles under her eyes and her red streaked face gave her away. Savanah had never looked so old to her daughter before, and the sight startled her with a twinge of discomfort.

"So when is he coming?" Kara started, in a near whisper that still held a hint of antagonism. "I want to meet my brother!"

It took all the emotional strength remaining within Savannah to open her mouth and form the words. "About two hours," came a barely audible voice. Savannah bolted from the room, down the hallway and into the bathroom. The door closed, and Kara heard the sound of running water. Then to her astonishment, she heard what sounded like someone vomiting violently.

Though a portion of Kara started to feel a bit sorry for her mother, she quickly pushed the thoughts away. The resentment that engulfed her mind left no room for compassion. "Serves her right," she contemplated. "It's about time she feel bad. She has ruined my life! I hope she feels a lot worse before this is over. I hope she can't eat for a month!" Kara's heart skipped a beat and her breath felt heavy when she heard the doorbell screech through the house. Surely it wasn't him already. Mom had said two hours, and it had only been fifteen minutes. Her hands were cold and clammy as she grabbed the knob and opened the door.

In front of her stood a tall, thin, young man with blonde curly hair. His eyes shone of blazing blue, and he donned a bit of an inviting smile on his face. Those eyes looked like he had never frowned in his life. He wore a well pressed, white dress shirt and light blue jeans that looked as though they had never been worn. Even his white tennis shoes looked perfectly clean. The appearance of this boy held no resemblance to the images conjured up in Kara's mind from the angry voice on the phone.

"Hi," he began in a pleasantly quiet voice. "You must be Kara. I am Jeremy. Mo...," he paused. "I mean, Savannah told me about you. So you are my sister? I am sorry I was so rude to you on the phone. It's just that I only found out I was adopted a few months ago, when my adopted parents were killed in a car accident, and I never dreamed I had a sister. It was so hard to track down Mo.. I mean, Savannah." Kara stood motionless. "Can I come in?" Moving aside, Kara allowed the boy to enter the room. Her mind raced. He had to be six foot tall, the way he towered over her five-foot-two frame. "Is Savannah here?"

Still seething with resentment, she answered the boy. "Yeah, maybe she'll come out when she figures out how to tell time. She said you'd be here in two hours."

"I am early," the boy continued, ignoring the curtness of her reply. "Guess I wanted to talk to my sister, too." He smiled that amazing smile.

Kara astounded herself when she asked, "Want to go up to my room?" It sounded utterly ridiculous, like a school girl flirting with a boy she had never met. Where did that come from, and why had she been so forward with the boy?

"Sure," came the equally shocking reply. "If it's okay with Mo.. I mean, with Savannah."

"You can call her Mom if you like. I have had the use of that name all my life, and I don't think I will use it anymore. I'm sick of it. All yours," continued Kara's sarcastic dialogue. "And you can come up to my room. I really don't care if she likes it or not. I want to show you my art." She paused, then resumed her speech. "I have wanted a brother all my life. Everyone knew that. But they just pretended you didn't exist. I don't care what they want anymore."

"I am sorry, Kara," continued his hushed tone as he started up the stairs behind her. "I never intended to cause you so much pain."

"It's not your fault! You can't help the fact that your mother gave you away to hide the fact that she was a whore!"

Anger flashed in the boy's eyes, and he stopped in his tracks, firmly grabbing her shoulders and turning her to face him. The boy's smile vanished. "Don't you ever say anything like that about our mother again! If you weren't my sister, I'd … just don't ever say that again!" Jeremy walked to the couch and sat down. "I am not going up to your room until I see our mother!"

"Whatever," mumbled Kara, hiding the fear and humiliation in her heart. She would not show him anything now no matter what he said. Her art was too precious to waste on him now, too much of an expression of herself to share with him at this point. Kara walked to the bathroom door and yelled, "Your son is here!" Then she raced up stairs, went into her room, and pulled out her paints. Pulling out a brush, she painted one angry green stroke on her painting. Putting the brush into the cup of water she kept in the room, Kara flopped onto the bed and went to sleep.

....

Savannah gathered her thoughts after the abrupt announcement. Quickly washing her face with cool water and drying it, she looked in the mirror one last time. There was no way to hide the redness, not exactly how she wanted to present herself the first time she saw her son. Pushing her brown curls from her face, she crept towards the living room where her boy sat. Her eyes rested upon the neatly groomed, blonde youth who looked so much like the boy who briefly captured her emotions years ago, just before he left her life forever. And those eyes! Those beautiful blue eyes that had stolen her breath and made her chest flutter were gazing up at her again. Without thinking, Savannah ran to the boy and snatched him into her arms in one giant embrace. She was sobbing uncontrollably.

"I'm sorry, Mom," the boy started softly. "Is it ok if I call you Mom? I'm sorry I was so mean to you on the phone. I just figured you never wanted me. It's ok. I grew up in a nice home. I was just mad because they never told me about you." Hesitantly, he continued, "But I have to ask … I mean, well... Can you tell me about my father?"

"You look just like him," she responded hoarsely, "just like I remember him so many years ago, before I was pregnant with you, and before he left me. You have his eyes and his smile. His name was Jake Meyers. I never saw him again after you were born." Savannah hesitated, overwhelmed by the polite young man before her. In the voice of a girl much younger than herself, she started to cry. "Mother said there was no room for a baby. N…no room. T…too much trouble." Stammering, she squeaked out the words, "I thought that your father was the nicest man I had ever met, but he left. I thought he was rescuing me, but it didn't last long. Mother tried to force me have an abortion. She took me to an abortionist to do it, but I kicked and screamed so loud for the doctor that he got mad and would not do the procedure. She was so angry." Savannah took a deep breath. "I had never defied her quite like that before. I thought she would just leave me there to stay on the street. But instead she grabbed me by the hair and threw me into my uncle's car. At home she took a belt to me. It seemed she would never stop. A couple of times she hit my belly. I was afraid she'd kill you. Then she screamed that if I was stupid enough to have you, she'd give you away. She said if I tried to stop her, she'd kill us both. I thought your father would help me, but when I told him, he just… well, he wouldn't do anything. I had to run away. So when you were born, I hurried to an orphanage and gave you away myself. I was afraid she'd sell you for drugs or something. You were so beautiful! You were all I had left of your father, and I wanted you so much!" Savannah gasped, covering her mouth, as she looked up at the boy who was listening in horror. It had just all tumbled out of her. She had never told anyone that story, not even David. And here she was, telling all these sordid details to her polite young son. "I'm sorry! I'm so sorry! You didn't need to know all that! I didn't mean to tell you all that! It's just that I've spent this whole night reliving the nightmare. I am so sorry!"

"It's ok, Mom. I did need to know that," Jeremy responded gently. "I needed to know that someone fought that hard to keep me alive. I've asked God about that so many times over the past few months, asking why nobody wanted me." There were tears in the boy's eyes.

Savannah's ears perked up. She could barely believe what she was hearing. "So… so you've found Jesus too? God answered my prayers, and you know Him too?" A bit of hope surged through her being, and she desperately needed it answered. Before he could respond, she added, "Of course I wanted you! I felt like there was no other choice!"

"Yes, I met Jesus three years ago, and I've prayed for you ever since I knew you existed. Thanks for praying for me, Mom. I love you, and I forgive you. Will you forgive me too? I was so mean to you on the phone. I don't usually talk to people that way!"

A wave of healing flooded Savannah's heart, a comfort she had never felt in her entire life. At least her son loved her. Her heart felt light, if just for this moment. "Of course I forgive you, but I really don't feel like I have anything to forgive you for." She paused. "You met Kara?"

"Yes. I think she's pretty mad at me though. I kind of lost my temper with her when she said something mean about you. Sorry. I know she is hurt too."

Even amidst the new hope, Savannah felt the stabbing in her heart for Kara. "She's pretty angry with everyone right now. Just give her time. Will you keep coming to visit us?"

Jeremy was the one nearly gasping with emotion this time. "If you'll have me, Mom. If you'll have me, no one will keep me away again!" Mother and son embraced, weeping together for some time. They were forming a bond that would endure for a lifetime.

....

Glancing over the pile of papers on his desk, David could not concentrate on his work. The office had always been a refuge before when things were tough, a welcome distraction. But this was different. He knew that the boy was coming to his house while he was at work today. Though he was glad to be away and not see the boy himself, he could barely control the seething anger within him. It poisoned his thoughts and filled his entire being. His coworkers were too busy to notice the fiery rage in his dark brown eyes, those eyes that looked almost black with anger. How dare this boy disrupt their lives like this! And the nerve of Savannah to answer him the way she had, refusing to keep that boy away from Kara! The kid was probably dangerous, maybe a sexual pervert. David refused to even think of the boy's name. No, he was just that boy. Any name made him too much of a person.

David was still reeling from Kara's tongue lashing the day before. He tried to think of a way to help Kara blame this entire situation on Savannah rather than on himself. Nothing came to his mind. It had to be Savannah's fault. He was not the one who had a baby outside of marriage. No, it was her fault, and he and Kara were suffering in the aftermath of Savannah's sin. It was plain and simple. It was her fault. His mother was right. Why did he ever marry her?

Fumbling through a few papers on his desk, David did as much as he could manage. Savannah had him so upset he could not work correctly. He came across a scribbled note, a scripture reference. 2 Corinthians 5:17 "Therefore if anyone [is] in Christ, [he is] a new creation: old things have passed away; behold, all things have become new." (NKJV) David hastily threw the paper into the trash. Brushing away the twinge of conviction, his angry thoughts continued. She had a choice! A sixteen year old has a choice! She probably did not even know who the father was! She probably slept with every man on the street! Why had he married someone who used to be a whore? His wife seemed so dirty to him now.

Acquiescing only slightly, David decided to be civil with Savannah and merely refrain from discussing the situation for now, as long as that boy stayed away. This had better be the boy's only visit, he decided. After all, God surely could not expect more than that. David felt a little better. He was doing a good thing, tolerating his wife's behavior. Sipping his cold coffee, he scarcely noticed the taste. It was time for a lunch break already. Hearing a voice behind him, David jumped a bit, startled away from his internal dialogue. It was Jack, and this would be a welcome interruption any other day. "Ready for lunch?" the man asked.

"A little behind right now," he replied, sure that he could not sustain a happy front for an hour and unwilling to confide in the man. "Think I'll skip it today," he continued, a smile plastered across his face. Jack left, and David trudged not too successfully through the rest of the shift. He was relieved that there were no more human interactions that demanded this performance for the remainder of his time at work. At least the accounting figures before him required no more than a bit of stale deliberation, and he could complete his tasks mechanically. It proved to be a difficult day.

....

Kara had fallen asleep after the confrontation with her brother. She was having that dream again. She was a little girl, running and running, clutching an old Barbie doll. The tall man with dark hair was chasing her again. He kept getting closer, yelling menacingly for her to stop. His arms were so close to her that she could see the ugly open sores all over them. He seemed like a monster, and the smells overpowered her. The man reeked of sweat, alcohol, tobacco, and even vomit. Though she had never been around alcohol before, somehow in the dream she recognized the scent. She nearly gagged as he reached for her, his unwashed black hair in clumps. Kara shook herself as hard as she could and barely woke up before the man's hands touched her.

She sat up in bed, soaked with perspiration, struggling to remove the twisted sheets from her face. At least it was light in the room, as she had entered her slumber in the day time. Kara wondered how long she had been sleeping but was too disoriented to look at her clock. She sat there frozen again. She wanted to paint her dream, to allow someone else to experience the darkness with her, the terror that she could not understand. But as she became more awake, she could no longer remember the details of the nightmare. She just knew it was a very bad dream. Kara wondered if Jeremy had left yet. Surely he would be gone before Dad came back. How dare he talk to her like that! Who did he think he was? He did not even know Savannah (true to her word, Kara determined to reserve the term Mom for Jeremy's private use). How dare he tell her how to talk about the woman! He had not spent the last fifteen years living with the stupid creature! Maybe Dad was right to keep them apart. Maybe he already knew what Jeremy was like. Still, he should have told her. No, he certainly was not off the hook.

A new darkness had settled over Kara's soul. Strangely in her rage, she found comfort in that place. It was a place she could go and hide away, a place where she could think all the thoughts of anger and hatred she desired. In this secret closet, Kara did not have to make excuses for her feelings. She did not care if they were evil, and the only person that was important was her. No one else was invited into this chamber. Though a bit of despair crept in with this darkness, Kara decided to consider these feelings her friends. No one could stop her here. She decided that here, and only here, she was in complete control. She could sin openly in this shelter if she desired, as Kara was convinced that even God could not see her here. Yes, it was despair, sweet despair.

Psalms 139:8 "If I ascend into heaven, You are there; If I make my bed in hell, behold, You are there." (NKJV)

Chapter 2

Weeks had elapsed with very few words exchanged between Savannah and her daughter. Savannah's heart sank as she heard Kara call her by her first name rather than addressing her as Mom. Even David barely spoke anymore, and he did nothing to discourage Kara's disrespect. He was mostly polite, though quite superior to her personage. A thick blanket of darkness enveloped them all in a sullen lifeless state. To unknowing witnesses, life went on as usual. There were no harsh tones, no arguments, nothing. Only a keen observer would notice the lack of laughter and the vacuum of emotion where hugs and kisses once lived.

Drained by the massive flow of passion preceding this blackness, Savannah scheduled an appointment with the doctor. Perhaps her hormones were off. She could not shake the depression that had overcome her. Savannah had lost her voice to pray. Each time she opened her mouth, the words were snatched from her. Perhaps the words were never there at all. She was convinced that something had to change, and at this point, even absolute disaster would be an improvement. The darkness of her thoughts convinced her that without help, she would not survive long. Savannah was drowning in an avalanche of despair with no strength to try to rescue herself.

Jeremy called occasionally but was afraid to visit, as David had told him in no uncertain terms to stay away, especially from

Kara. His scattered contacts were the only brightness in Savannah's life. She hated the fact that Kara could not share in this bit of comfort, but her daughter was so angry that she refused any opportunity to talk to the boy. Savannah's concern about Kara was transitioning into complete dread of what would happen next. She was convinced that Kara was not sleeping well, as her bedroom light stayed on most of the night. Even her overall countenance had darkened, and she seemed to be slipping more and more into an unreachable cavern of hopelessness. How could she help her children? She desired so deeply to mother the son that she had been forced to give away and to protect the daughter she loved so much, and she was sure she was inadequate for either. She was convinced that nothing could ever be made right again.

Savannah also lamented the loss of the close fellowship she had with her Heavenly Father, the only father she had ever known, as she felt He would not follow her here into this darkness. Maybe she was not really completely forgiven for her past after all. Perhaps this was her time to pay for the sins of yesterday. None of it matched what she had been taught, but everything was upside down in her life right now. Savannah longed painfully for the days when she had sat, visualizing herself in the lap of Jesus, held firmly in His embrace. There they would talk about practically anything. They had been such good friends. She told Him everything, and nothing in her life seemed insignificant to Him. Yet somehow this closeness had never transferred to any human relationships. Why hadn't she been able to discuss her most painful memories even with David? Was not marriage a picture of the perfect relationship with God? A new dread crept over Savannah as she feared she would have to explain to David about the abortion she had been forced to have. These hurts were so deep that she felt terror in the thought of trying to put them into words. No language could ever explain the horrors, and she felt the words would literally tear up her throat if she let them escape. Savannah was sure that no one could even faintly fathom what was in her unless they had lived it with her. This was particularly solidified in the face of the recent happenings in her life.

Thinking on these things, Savannah wept bitterly. It was not hard to get alone to cry anymore, as everyone avoided her like the plague, everyone except Jeremy, that is. He would call, but she could not see him. This was especially painful, as she felt he needed her now that his adopted parents were dead. Amidst all this, however, was the utterly amazing fact that he seemed to have come out of this the most unscathed, having truly found his refuge in Jesus Christ, his Savior and Friend. Perhaps the fact that Jeremy had forgiven her was proof that God still loved her a little bit. He had answered her prayers that the boy would have a relationship with the Lord, and He had done it in such a magnificent way. Her mother-in-law could not offer her constant jabs, as she presently had nothing to do with Savannah. This was a sort of bitter-sweet fact, accompanied by the pain associated with the awareness of the numerous words spoken between mother and son to bring this about, as well as the knowledge that David was far from defending her.

Picking up her Bible, she tried in vain to rest her eyes upon a scripture… anything that would give her direction or comfort. Savannah could not focus to read more than a couple of words, of which she could make no sense. She laid the Bible down beside her and dozed in the chair into a fitful sleep filled with familiar nightmares of what had been. Though the dreams had vanished for several years following her conversion, they had made their way back again, furiously haunting her very soul. She could never run fast enough, never fight hard enough, to get HIM off of her. She nearly gagged on her own vomit as his mouth covered hers, the stench of alcohol overpowering her. The pain was as intense in her dreams as if it were actually occurring again, her skin tearing with each penetration, her body recoiling each time he struck her for making a sound. His sneer was permanently etched into her mind. "Happy Birthday," he would growl. "You are a woman now!" She relived it over and over in full detail, tormented by what had been.

....

David and Kara started out the door. A visit to Grandma's seemed a comic relief for the grandchild, as she somewhat gloated in her new awareness of Grandma's disapproval of Savannah. She determined to set the conversation towards the woman she used to call Mom at any opportunity that presented itself, hoping to stir up any negative remarks. Though she was usually somewhat disappointed by Grandma's surprising ability to hold her tongue in

Kara's presence, she reveled in the few quips she could incite. It somehow gave her a sense of supremacy, though she had to guard that pleasure, letting it express itself only in that dark closet she had created in her life. That was the place where hatred and sin could express itself freely, and Kara visited it so frequently now in her alone time that she rarely bothered to talk to God. She was mad at Him anyway and felt that He, like her parents, really did not understand her. He, like all adults, had betrayed her.

The twenty mile trip progressed rapidly by, with Kara occasionally humoring David with a bit of light conversation. She felt she could pretend, at least, to not be entirely furious with him. She saved most of the toxic emotions for her alone time and for any unwanted interactions with Savannah. Kara determined that Savannah would not enjoy the same luxury as David in this way, as her anger towards the woman was too intense for that. Maybe if Savannah had not made her so mad, she wouldn't have set Jeremy off the way she did, and they might still be talking. As it was, however, her pride was too deeply damaged to even consider making room for a relationship with her brother.

Lost in her thoughts, Kara did not even notice the greenery about her, as the road wound through a beautiful neighborhood, decorated with flowers of every color. She could have seen the hues of her paints scattered throughout nature, as well as some colors she could never quite mix, but her state of mind prevented it. The area gave off an air of quiet peace that had always brought comfort to David's soul. This was his place of refuge, his memory of more perfect days without the clutter of troublesome events. This was where he grew up, sheltered from chaos, where he had always known that God was real, though he rarely felt the need to pursue Him much on a personal level. He had accepted Jesus as a child and confirmed his decision in his early teens, but it had always been easy to depend on the care of his parents as a child and on his good job as an adult. These troubles with Savannah had darkened the picture of late, but he knew he could always come back here. He did spend some time in prayer, at least until all these things occurred, and he loved God in the only way he knew how; but the intimate relationship he had heard Savannah talk about seemed to elude him. Perhaps that was just what emotional woman experienced, he considered. Men were not really like women. They were better equipped to take care of themselves. Besides, look where this wonderful relationship Savannah claimed to have, had gotten them. Maybe it was all a fake, something Savannah invented to comfort herself in her guilt. David was at least relieved that Kara was talking to him a little bit again. Perhaps she understood that this really was all Savannah's fault, a result of Savannah's sin. Perhaps it was not necessary for him to convince her of that after all.

As the car pulled into Grandma's driveway, both father and daughter experienced the warmth of the small red brick house with a large green tree out front, shading the extravagantly green lawn. The roses fairly reached out to embrace them, and for a brief moment, they both forgot darkness had fallen upon them. Grandma met them at the door with her usual cheery disposition on seeing her son, though she appeared a bit guarded at first until she looked about to see whether or not Savannah was in the car as well. Satisfied that she needed only entertain her two favorite people, she escorted them into the house, where they were met with the aroma of cinnamon and apple. To their delight, she was baking a pie.

David sat in the big brown arm chair, and Kara rested on a comfy old couch covered with an old orange and white afghan, while Grandma finished preparing the meatloaf that was David's favorite, with corn, mashed potatoes, and gravy. David sighed as he reflected on the fact that he could relax here anytime... anytime, that is, when Savannah was not in the picture, when he did not have to feel guilty for not defending her. Now, of course, he would feel no such compulsion anyway. And he had Kara with him to enjoy it as well. It always amazed David how perfect it seemed to be at home with Mom. Sure, he missed his dad, who had died of a heart attack a year ago. But at least he always had Mom. There was something soothing and safe in that.

From the kitchen, Grandma proceeded to ask the pair how things were. She had determined to keep Savannah out of the conversation for Kara's sake, but Kara had other plans. "Better since I have been too busy to spend time with Savannah," Kara remarked. "Dad and I are doing fine. Savannah is so busy moping around the house until Jeremy calls that we get to do other things. I get to paint a lot."

Kara was disappointed when Grandma ignored her references to Savannah. Grandma was a bit disturbed to hear the child refer to her mother by her first name but thought, what can you expect? She is feeling betrayed by the woman. David and Savannah's marriage had always been a thorn in her side. Still she was determined to avoid feeding Kara's defiance. "So what are you painting?" she replied.

"Just pictures," came Kara's disappointed answer. "Nothing much."

"She spends hours painting," continued David. "I am sure her paintings are fabulous by now."

If only he knew, Kara mused. Her paintings were getting darker and darker, and she was sure he would be displeased if he saw them. They had become a part of that dark world, that place of sin and despair where she sought refuge. Let him think they are good, she thought. She was not going to show them to anyone anyway, at least not for a long while.

"Let's eat," Grandma continued, "while it is still hot." The three enjoyed their meal and time together, savoring the taste of the meatloaf, the vegetables, and especially the pie that followed, while Grandma worked to keep the conversation on a lighter level. Grandma refused help with the cleanup, and they spent the rest of the afternoon relaxing and talking. At one point, Grandma pulled out a familiar board game, additionally lightening the mood of the day. Though she was a bit bored, Kara was happy just to have a place to be. She was still ready, however, when early evening brought Dad's decision to leave.

The three hugged and kissed goodbye, and as she was walking to the car, Kara overheard Grandma talking to Dad. "How long are you going to put up with that woman's antics? I wish you had listened to me sixteen years ago when I told you not to marry her! She has really shown herself up in this, David." Dad said nothing and walked back to the car. Kara took a sinister pleasure in Grandma's words, and father and daughter were on their way again.

Kara dozed off during the ride home. She still felt the comfort of Grandma's smile and was glad they had spent time with her. Even the dark feelings lifted a bit, giving her a brief reprieve. Once home, she scampered into the house and quickly up to her room. Grandma's lunch had satisfied her enough that she decided not to brave the trip downstairs for supper. Why spoil the mood?

The respite was short lived, however, as all the black thoughts began to race about her mind again. It was time for her secret place. Securing the lock on her bedroom door, Kara sat on the floor with her paints. She turned her music up loud and closed her blinds. This was her one great comfort, her art. She pushed away the pile of soiled clothes and glanced at the dirty plate and cup on her night stand. The room was cramped at best, especially with the clutter, but this was Kara's world. Summer had forced her to hibernate, but soon school would start again. Even the thought of seeing friends offered little solace. Her life had now morphed into this cheerless existence.

There it was, the clanging of the phone throughout the house. How dare that tone interrupt her concentration! She let it continue to ring, but no one was answering it. Annoyed by the tone, she decided to respond. She turned the music down. "Hello."

"Savannah? Is this Savannah Tells?" Why had she picked up the phone? Kara certainly did not want to take the phone downstairs to Savannah.

Not quite sure why, Kara replied, "Yes it is. How can I help you?" She nearly laughed at her own cleverness.

"This is Dr. Crestoff's office returning your call. You wanted to make an appointment?"

"Yes please, as soon as possible. I haven't been feeling well." Kara had no idea what the appointment was for but was convinced this would suffice.

"We just need to update our records. You are thirty-six years old, right?"

"Yes." This was actually fun. She could make up any answers she wanted.

"Married?"

"No, divorced," Kara held back a snicker. Besides, at the rate things were going, maybe it would be true soon.

"That may change your insurance status."

"No," Kara responded quickly. "Actually the divorce is not final yet." That was a close one!

"Number of living children?"

"Two, but only one living with me."

"Just to clarify, our records state you had a late term abortion as well? And it says here that it was preformed in a non-sterile

42

environment? I am sorry I have to bring up the subject, but it seems the physician who delivered your last child felt that the damage done by this procedure resulted in your need for a hysterectomy after your last child's birth." Kara felt her breath nearly escape her. "Just a legal issue, mam. You understand. He needs to document these things, with malpractice and all."

Kara gathered her composure. "Yes, of course. Did they record the sex of the.. uh.. fetus?"

"Oh yes. It was a girl, right? Yes, here it is. Not that it really makes any difference. We don't need to bring up any more of that memory."

"Oh, I'd nearly forgotten it," was the curt reply. "Do you need anything else?" Was this lady an idiot? She was divulging all this information over the phone! What made her so sure she was Savannah? Even that name was hateful to her now.

"Think we've got most of it. Oh. Ever been diagnosed with any sexually transmitted diseases? I don't see that on here."

"Oh yes. Herpes. And gonorrhea I think. It's been treated though."

"Any recent herpes outbreak? Oh, and are you presently taking any medications?"

"No, no outbreaks, and I am not on any medications. Oh, and this is confidential, right? I don't tell my family about these things."

The voice went silent for a moment. "Mam, I have a signed release from you stating that we can discuss your records with your husband. Do you want to change that?"

Kara felt a slight pang of guilt. "Yes please." Her anger overcame her reason, however. "He doesn't need to know my private information, especially with the divorce and all. Besides, I am seeing another man."

"We will call you back with an appointment time, Savannah. We will try to fit you into our schedule within the next two days. Thank you, and goodbye."

"Goodbye."

The room became a swirl of shapeless colors. Nothing made any sense. Her sister… her sister… dead… murdered. It had all been a lie. Her whole life was a lie. Kara could not calm her thoughts. She thought she had hated …That Woman… before, but this was beyond comprehension. That Woman did not even deserve a name. This could never be forgiven if she lived a thousand lifetimes. Overwhelmed with the passions of her thoughts, Kara fell back on the bed into a heavy slumber.

....

Why was this happening? How could she make it stop? It was that dream again! She was a littler girl hiding in a closet, clutching an old, ragged Barbie doll. She had an urgent need to go to the bathroom but was afraid to leave her corner. The air was stale, and loud music blared in the background. People were laughing and conversing wildly. Someone was arguing.

The child peered around the corner of the closet door, and seeing no one, ran down a dark hallway into a side bathroom. It was dark and smelled worse than any bathroom Kara had ever visited. Tiny pieces of aluminum foil were everywhere, and the smudged mirror revealed the frame of a girl about twelve, unkempt with a dirt streaked face. After making careful search of her surroundings, the child bolted back down the hall. She gave a sigh of relief as she entered the room with the closet. But as she placed her hand upon the door to open it, the most horrific odor filled her nostrils, and a filthy hand came from behind her, grabbing her and covering her mouth. "Happy Birthday," he growled, calling her a name that Kara couldn't quite hear. "You are twelve years old today, and I got your birthday present. You're a woman now, and you know what that means. Time to take your place in this house. Don't you dare make a sound!" And he pulled her to the floor.

It was him! The filthy man with the awful smells and clumped black hair! He had her! Why hadn't she woken up? Kara squirmed and pulled with all her might and woke out of her fitful sleep, sheets wound tightly about her face. Fighting to free herself of the bedding, her heart was pounding in her throat, and she could still taste the dirt on the man's hand. She could not catch her breath, and her entire body was saturated with perspiration.

Kara decided this was enough. The antics of That Woman were driving her crazy. She had to leave. She had to run away. Still dazed, she threw some clothes in an overnight bag, not really thinking about what she would need or what she would do next. The sun had gone down while she was asleep, and it was dark in the room. The details of the nightmare were fading, but the terror remained.

Where could she go? Gathering her little phone book, Kara thumbed through the pages. There it was, the one name she could call! She had to do something! This house was driving her crazy! She barely felt her fingers move to dial before hearing a ring on the other end. "Hello," he answered.

"Yeah, Daniel, it's Kara."

"Haven't heard from you in a while, cutie. What's up?"

"Not much," the words echoed hollowly. "Just thought I'd say hi. Nothing to do."

"Kind of late for a little Christian girl. After seven o'clock, you know," continued the sarcastic tone.

"I don't know anyone like that, but if you don't want to talk, I'll hang up!"

"No! Don't hang up! Want to go for a ride? I can be there in thirty minutes."

"Sure, I got nothing to do. But don't ring the bell. I'll meet you outside. See you in a bit."

"I'll be there."

Kara grabbed a piece of paper and pencil and scribbled a brief note. No one deserved more than that, not in this house at least, and especially not That Woman.

STRANGER WHO KEPT ME IN THIS PRISON OF LIES ALL
THESE YEARS:

YOU MIGHT WANT TO CALL YOUR DOCTOR'S OFFICE
FOR YOUR APPOINTMENT. IT WOULD ALSO BE A GOOD
IDEA TO TELL THEM NOT TO ASK YOU INFORMATION
OVER THE PHONE. PEOPLE FIND OUT YOUR LIES THAT
WAY. THOUGH YOU DON'T DESERVE AN EXPLANATION,
THINK I'LL TRY TO FIND A STONE FOR MY SISTER'S
UNMARKED GRAVE. OH YEAH. NEVER MIND. YOU
PROBABLY JUST THREW HER BODY AWAY! YOU
KNOW..... THEY CALLED IT A "LATE TERM ABORTION"?
NOT SURE WHEN YOU WERE PLANNING TO TELL ME
ABOUT THAT! OH YEAH, NEVER?

NOT COMING BACK, BY THE WAY.

KARA

Kara felt an intense sense of satisfaction as she laid the note
on her pillow. Peering out of her room, she could see that no one
was in sight of the stairs. Down the hall a light shown under That
Woman's bedroom door. Kara crept down the stairs, around the
corner, and out the front door silently into the night.

Daniel's car was in front of the house within twenty minutes.
Climbing into the front seat, Kara smelled the strong aroma of

alcohol. How did she know that was what it was? It was oddly familiar. A boy and two girls she did not know were in the rear seat. Smoke was rolling out of the back of the car from their cigarettes, and the radio was blaring. The other boy was kissing a thin blond girl, and a full figured red headed beauty was putting on makeup. "We got to go get Missy's date," began the voice behind the steering wheel. "Better find a seatbelt, little Christian girl. Mommy and Daddy might be watching! Hey, what's with the bag? Bring enough clothes to stay out with us all night? Might turn into a pumpkin!"

The back seat was filled with cackles and snickering. Kara angrily dropped the seat belt she had started to fasten. "Knock it off! Just not going home tonight!"

"Ooooooh," proceeded from the backseat.

Daniel handed Kara an open bottle of beer. Raising it to her lips, she pulled it back. It was that smell! She had wanted so badly to do this to spite That Woman, but the scent was too intensely familiar. "No thanks," escaped her throat. She was furious. She couldn't even sin correctly!

"Take the little Christian girl back home!" retorted Missy. "We don't need her kind of trouble!"

"She'll be okay," proclaimed Daniel. "She'll be just fine." Kara felt a bit uneasy with the reply but ignored it.

The car halted in front of a tiny, weather beaten house. Shingles were falling from the roof. The grass was overgrown, and weeds were scattered at frequent intervals throughout the yard. Out sauntered a tall, skinny young man. His shoulder length brown hair

48

moved with his stride. He was dressed in a black t-shirt and old jeans.

"Wanna drive?" asked Daniel. The girl with the makeup crawled over the seat into the front, nearly sitting on Kara. Opening Kara's door, Daniel encouraged Kara to get in the back seat with him. "You can sit on my lap. Too crowded up here."

Displaced by Missy's rudeness, it seemed the best move at the time, and Kara obliged. Even the smoke and alcohol was better than her surly remarks, and she was determined not to go home.

As the vehicle propelled down the road, Kara felt Daniel's hand slipping under her shirt and beneath her bra. Before she had time to object, his mouth was covering hers, and she could not get free of his grasp. The couple in the back with them were laughing, and the other boy pinned one of her arms to the seat as Daniel sat on the other. Within seconds, Daniel began loosening her pants. She was frantic! This was reminding her of something horrific, though she was not sure what. The panic within her empowered her in a way that shocked even Daniel, and just as she was freeing herself, she heard the loudest bang and set of screams she had heard in her life. She was weightless, flying through something with a stinging sensation nearly everywhere on her body. Kara's leg began to throb, and she felt the impact of her weight striking concrete. Everything was black as the air was filled with a mixture of panicked wails and the smell of blood and alcohol.

Kara could barely catch her breath. She was sure someone was stepping on her chest. The sounds of sirens pierced the night, and voices were everywhere, though none were comprehensible. Her thoughts slowly faded as she drifted farther and farther into the darkness. "Is this what it feels like to die?" she mused.

....

David was startled out of a sound slumber. It was three in the morning. Why was he awake? Not sure what had startled him, he sensed a sort of foreboding, far more ominous than the darkness that had settled over the house this summer. Leaping from the bed, he raced up the stairs to Kara's room. The door was ajar, and the light was off. David crept in quietly in case she was asleep, but the small frame of his daughter was not on the bed.

As the light from the lamp filled the room, David observed the clutter strewn throughout Kara's abode. Clothes and even a few dirty dishes were scattered everywhere. Then his eyes lit on the small piece of paper resting on her pillow. The aroma of lilacs, Kara's favorite perfume, filled the air. It was the perfume he had purchased for her birthday. Reading the note, he froze. This was more than he could process. Flashing images of little Kara running to him, grabbing him, giving Daddy a kiss.... the sounds of her little giggles....the afternoon with Grandma... even the echo of her angry words were a bittersweet torment in David's mind.

Gazing about the room, one of Kara's paintings caught David's notice. It was mostly black with faint images of people bleeding and dying. There were creatures of dark green dispersed among the bleeding people, and the blackness of the painting overwhelmed him. The green creatures seemed to be sneering at him. David felt ill at what he saw. Why hadn't he noticed this darkness over his daughter's life? He pushed away a twinge of guilt at having been so involved in his own anger that he did not notice what was happening to Kara. These feelings were replaced immediately by his immense rage at the words he had read and the woman he felt was responsible.

Hearing David's abrupt ascent, Savannah arose from bed to see what was taking place. At the top of the stairs he stood, motionless. As she reached him, he threw the paper at Savannah. The words left her stunned beyond comprehension.

David looked at his wife. Savannah's sins had destroyed them. This was more than he could bear. "An abortion! You murdered a child! And you didn't even have the decency to tell me! Now look what you have done to our child… MY child! You destroy everything in your path!" Savannah couldn't move or speak. David's entire being was filled with a rage neither of them had ever known, and he barely felt his arm move before the force of the slap across Savannah's face landed, stronger than he would have ever hit any man. Savannah was slung across the floor to the bed, hitting her face against the frame.

Savannah clutched the side of the bed to lift herself to her feet. A fear from long ago encompassed her being as she prepared to exit the room. David had never hit a woman in his life, and neither or them knew what was coming next. "Get out!" he growled. "Go back to your old life!" He followed her menacingly down the steps, barely controlling the motion of his hands at his side. As Savannah picked up her purse, he snatched it from her. David grabbed her wallet and removed the money and credit cards, then threw the empty case back into her purse. After taking away her cell phone, he threw the purse back at her. "Get out! And don't ever come back!"

David watched his wife as she entered the night. Seething in his hatred, he was relieved to never see her again. The man collapsed onto his bed and fell into his own set of nightmares.

....

The man awoke with a start. "David!" exclaimed the stern Voice. "What have you done?" A certain terror crept over his soul as he remembered the events of the previous hours. Where was Kara? Had he actually hit Savannah? Surely it was just a bad dream. He had never hit anyone like that, much less a woman and one he loved. Loved? The torrent of fury again overwhelmed him until he knew the memory was true. "David!" resonated the Voice, more severe than before. His entire being quaked at the sound.

David wondered if he was really awake. He heard a feeble sound arise from within him. "Yes, Lord?"

"What have you done? Where are My children tonight?"

David could scarcely catch his breath. He was terrified to answer. Excuses were unthinkable. This was David and God. He dare not remotely consider a scapegoat. Words fled his mind, leaving him with no reply.

"What have you done?" The Voice demanded, the fierceness escalating in David's gut. "Do you have no answer for these things?"

"Lord, You know," squeaked his frail voice. "I… hit… her."

Before the accusations against Savannah could even surface his thoughts, the Voice started again. "Two!" it thundered.

"Two what?" squeaked David's words again.

"Two, David. Two!" repeated the Voice, seemingly in a near shout. "You wanted to know how many men Savannah slept with before you! There were two! How many women were there for you? How many, David! Answer Me!"

"Three," gasped the shaken man. "Three, Lord."

"And shall I retain your sins?"

With amazing speed and accuracy, the words of Jesus flowed through his being. "Therefore is the kingdom of heaven likened unto a certain king, which would take account of his servants. And when he had begun to reckon, one was brought unto him, which owed him ten thousand talents. But forasmuch as he had not to pay, his lord commanded him to be sold, and his wife, and children, and all that he had, and payment to be made. The servant therefore fell down, and worshipped him, saying, Lord, have patience with me, and I will pay thee all. Then the lord of that servant was moved with compassion, and loosed him, and forgave him the debt. But the same servant went out, and found one of his fellowservants, which owed him an hundred pence: and he laid hands on him, and took [him] by the throat, saying, Pay me that thou owest. And his fellowservant fell down at his feet, and besought him, saying, Have patience with me, and I will pay thee all. And he would not: but went and cast him into prison, till he should pay the debt. So when his fellowservants saw what was done, they were very sorry, and came and told unto their lord all that was done. Then his lord, after that he had called him, said unto him, O thou wicked servant, I forgave thee all that debt, because thou desiredst me: Shouldest not thou also have had compassion on thy fellowservant, even as I had pity on thee? And his lord was wroth, and delivered him to the tormentors, till he should pay all that was due unto him. So likewise shall my heavenly Father do also unto you, if ye from your hearts forgive not every one his brother their trespasses." (Matthew 18:23-35 KJV)

The Voice thundered again, "Shall I retain your sins?"

"No, Lord, please. No!" he pled. "I forgive her! You sent me to rescue her, and I have failed! I am sorry, Lord!"

"Rescue her?" The Voice sounded almost annoyed, with a hint of laughter. "I rescued Savannah before she met you! She is Mine! I never sent you to rescue her! I sent Savannah to rescue you!"

"Me? From what?" David was incredulous. His life had been so perfect, free of the painful memories Savannah must have. Rescue him?

This time the voice boomed. If he had not been on the bed, he would surely have fallen. "From your own self righteousness, David! You are a Pharisee!"

This time David fell from the bed to the floor, cut to the very depths of his being. He sobbed uncontrollably for what seemed an eternity, weeping until no strength remained in Him. "Go!" proclaimed the Voice. "Go see the Scallians! You will find no rest until you know the truth, and your comfort will return only when you find Savannah! Go! You have work to do! I will speak no more to you on this matter until the task is complete!" At that point, a powerful yet gentle hand seemed to lift him back onto to the bed, and he fell asleep.

It seemed but a few minutes before David's eyes opened. Had it been a dream, or had God just spoken to him? His wet face and the terror in His soul left no room to doubt the vision. He knew what he must do, and he must do it now. Looking at the clock, he saw that it was nearly five, and the sun was rising over his home. David hardly noticed. Everything in him wanted to call the police, to find out where Kara was, but the vision was urgent. The Scallians were the Christian family that took Savannah in long ago. He had not seen them since Kara was three and wondered if they even lived in the same place.

The drive to the next town seemed unending. He passed what remained of a bad accident on the way. It seemed the police had experienced a busy night. Mansfield was only thirty miles away, with a road composed of winding and turning lanes. Palm trees scantly lined the desert road. There were no buildings in sight, and David remembered why he had stopped making this trip. It was such a deserted stretch of highway.

Ahead he recognized one lone structure. It was the home where he met Savannah so many years ago. He once again heard her girlish laughter. She had been such a free spirit, enthralled with the salvation of her King. What had happened? David winced as he heard the echo of the disapproving words of his mother, along with his own criticisms, hurled Savannah's way. He saw the sadness slip onto her face as she heard the cutting comments. What had he done? His heart became noticeably heavier, though that had not seemed possible. How could he repair the damage? He could only do what he had been instructed.

Pulling into the long country driveway, David noticed lights on in the kitchen. At least they were awake. Ignition off, his feet seemed set in quicksand as he pulled himself out of the car. How would he explain?

Robert Scallian walked out the door towards him. He was using a cane. David couldn't find his voice quickly enough to refrain the gentleman from his difficult assent down the three old porch steps and along the old stone walkway. Reaching out to clasp the white haired man's hand, he was pulled instead into a firm embrace. "I know why you are here," the old man whispered. "Savannah called me hours ago." He hesitated. "She called collect, said she didn't have money for a pay phone." Images of pulling the cash and credit cards out of Savannah's purse sent a horrified realization through David's being. He had sent her away penniless. She had no where to go. "She was hysterical, saying something about Kara and about you being insanely angry with her. Most of what she said didn't make much sense. She refused to come here, said she didn't have a ride anyway. Said she was going back to the streets because that is what you wanted. Savannah said she thought she would never see Kara again and that she could not bear to live anymore."

"David, she just kept rambling, sobbing as she begged us to forgive her for some backwoods abortion she never told us about. She kept repeating that her mother made her have the abortion so that her uncle who had raped her wouldn't go to jail. It was horrible, David. She kept saying that she was only twelve, that they ripped the baby out of her, and that she bled and bled. And the other part is so hard to think about, David. That baby tried to take a breath, but the abortionist placed his hands over the baby's face. She saw the baby in his hands and screamed behind the gag they put in her mouth to keep the neighbors from hearing what was happening. It was a little girl, David. She saw them murder her baby!"

David could no longer refrain himself. Falling to the ground, he sobbed with a violence that he did not know was in him. He lay for hours in the grass unable to move. How could he go on? He saw the very depths of his own wretchedness.

"O wretched man that I am! who shall deliver me from the body of this death? I thank God through Jesus Christ our Lord. ..." (Romans 7:24-24a KJV)

Chapter 3

Jeremy listened to the night sounds outside his window. The comforting tone of the crickets chirping reminded him that he was never truly alone. He missed the only parents he had ever known so very much. He had relinquished his initial anger that resulted from the discovery that they had hidden his adoption from him. His heart ached for those long talks with Dad, when they discussed everything from girls to money and college. Jeremy often regretted the decision not to further his education, but the money just was not there. He could still see the smile on his mother's face when he graduated from high school, and his heart ached as he remembered the events of that night. He had ridden home with a friend to attend another graduation party. When no one came to pick him up, he started calling. It was several hours before the police found him. His parents were already dead at that point, involved in a head on collision with a drunk driver. He was relieved that both of them had received Christ when he took them to church the week before, but an intense sadness fell upon him. This sorrow deepened and was mixed with anger when he was notified a week later that he had been adopted. His parents had left the information with their will. Most of the money they left him was consumed by funeral costs and existing bills, and within six months, all the money was gone.

It had been such a blessing to finally reunite with his birth mother and to discover that he had a sister, but the reunion was short lived, as Savannah's husband refused to allow him to visit their home. Though he often conversed with his newly found mother on the phone, it was just not the same. He mused over the phrase she spoke that had resulted in the adoption. "No room… for a baby". Yet he was reminded that there was no room for Jesus either, when He came. "Guess I am in good company," he thought, giving his pained heart a bit of rest. Here it was again, however. There was no room in his mother's family for him. His start with his sister was rocky as well, as she was so very angry to discover his existence. Though he knew the anger was due to discovering that he had been hidden from her, it still felt more like a personal rejection. Jeremy had decided not to attempt to contact his birth father, at least until his anger subsided to where he could be a witness to the man. He obviously had not wanted him anyway and had done nothing to protect him or his mother. Working through this anger and forgiveness would be a process, but he decided it would have to be done.

Jeremy's greatest comfort was his frequent talks with Jesus. There was an intense love in him for the One who had never deserted him, who had never let him down. He could always talk to Him, and he was frequently reminded that God was his true Father, a Father to the fatherless, who had rescued him when the world did not want him. Perhaps his adoption into His family proved his life to be a picture of something greater after all. Even with the rough start in his life, Jeremy knew he had much for which to be thankful. God had kept him alive when his grandmother insisted on killing him, and He placed him in a wonderful family. At least before the loss, He made sure that Jeremy knew the couple was safe in Him.

Thanking his Lord and worshipping Him as he lay upon his bed in his one bedroom apartment, Jeremy fell asleep.

Jeremy was awakened by a loud knock at the door. He looked at the clock. It was four thirty in the morning. Who could possibly want him at this hour? No one even knew where he lived except his new mother and the other residents in the building. The knock was insistent, so he climbed out of bed and threw some clothes on. When he opened the door a crack, he saw his mother standing there, so he let her in.

Jeremy was filled with horror at the sight. Her face was bruised, her mouth was bleeding, and she was crying hysterically. He made her a cup of tea, hoping to calm her enough for her to talk to him. A certain fury was rising up in him as he thought about the bruising on her face. Had someone hit her? He began to suspect David. No attempts to calm her seemed to work, and Jeremy debated on the wisdom of transporting her to a hospital. When he suggested it, however, she wildly shook her head. Finally she handed him a hand written note. It was written by his sister, Kara.

STRANGER WHO KEPT ME IN THIS PRISON OF LIES ALL THESE YEARS:

YOU MIGHT WANT TO CALL YOUR DOCTOR'S OFFICE FOR YOUR APPOINTMENT. IT WOULD ALSO BE A GOOD IDEA TO TELL THEM NOT TO ASK YOU INFORMATION OVER THE PHONE. PEOPLE FIND OUT YOUR LIES THAT

WAY. THOUGH YOU DON'T DESERVE AN EXPLANATION, THINK I'LL TRY TO FIND A STONE FOR MY SISTER'S UNMARKED GRAVE. OH YEAH. NEVER MIND. YOU PROBABLY JUST THREW HER BODY AWAY! YOU KNOW..... THEY CALLED IT A "LATE TERM ABORTION"? NOT SURE WHEN YOU WERE PLANNING TO TELL ME ABOUT THAT! OH YEAH, NEVER?

NOT COMING BACK, BY THE WAY.

KARA

A new rage rose up in the boy. So his grandmother had been successful in killing one baby! What kind of hell did his mother grow up in? And why hadn't someone taken the trouble to find out about her background and help her through these things? Why were they so quick to blame her? He was sure given the description of his own birth that Savannah had no choice in the matter. And even if she did, where had forgiveness gone? Holding Savannah firmly in his arms, he comforted her. She seemed unable to gather her thoughts enough to talk with him. Remembering what he told her at their first meeting, Jeremy felt he had let her down. "If you'll have me, no one will keep me away again!" he had told her. Why had he allowed David to block their relationship? Resigned to the fact that there would be no more sleep tonight, the two sat for hours, Savannah remaining in the arms of her young son. Though Savannah had calmed down some, she seemed unable still to articulate the happenings of the night, even as daylight landed. How like Christ in the midst of her trouble to hold Savannah through Jeremy when she could receive Him in no other way!

Another loud knock came at the door. Had David somehow found the place? Jeremy decided he was prepared for anything. Yet opening the door, he quickly discovered that he was sorely mistaken. The two policemen in front of him sent a start throughout his frame.

"Son, I am trying to locate Savannah Tells. Have you seen her?" asked a rather large man in a police uniform bearing a nametag that read Sergeant Merdail. "We have been trying to reach her and her husband for several hours." Without a sound, the boy escorted them in, completely unsure how all this would end. "Mam," the policeman addressed Savannah, casting a look of suspicion her way as he noted the bruising on her face, "we have been trying for hours to find you and your husband. There has been an accident involving several teenagers, and we need to find out if one of them is your daughter. Do you know where she is?"

Savannah shook her head, appearing more distraught than ever. "I think she took off," began Jeremy, showing the officer the note that Kara left. "I don't know where David is. Maybe he is out looking for her."

"How did your mother get those bruises, son?" the officer persisted.

"I really don't know, sir. I haven't been able to get her to talk since she got here."

"I need for you both to go the hospital with me," the officer continued coldly. "Do you have transportation, or do you need to ride with us? We need to find out who this little girl is. Why didn't anyone call when your sister came up missing?" he asked accusingly.

"I don't know why, sir, but I have no car," the boy responded. "I guess we should ride in your patrol car." Gathering Savannah in his arms, Jeremy escorted her to the police car and assisted her in. The fifteen minute drive was excruciatingly long, as Jeremy wondered what would come of all this. Was it Kara in the hospital? Was she even alive? A sick feeling settled within him. Savannah continued to sob, comforted only by her son.

The two were met by hospital staff, eager to identify the only breathing victim of this terrible accident. They were led to the side of the child, and Jeremy's heart sank as he saw Kara's mangled frame. Breathing only by the help of a respirator, the girl was barely alive. Savannah was so hysterical that no one could get any information from her. "It's her, officer," proceeded the words squeezed from the boy's throat. "I am sure it is her, though I have only seen her once." The officer gave him a peculiar look after the last response. "I just recently found out that I had a sister," he explained.

"We really need a parent for this, son. Is there any way to contact the girl's father?"

"I don't know, sir," he responded. He attempted to ask Savannah, who reached for a phone and dialed the only place she knew to call. She dialed the Scallions, the family that had rescued her so long ago. Perhaps they would know what to do. Hospital staff pulled the boy aside, explaining that it was unlikely Kara would survive more than a few hours. Jeremy's heart practically burst with pain as he heard his mother, barely comprehensible, attempt to explain her call. To his amazement, however, he could tell that David had come on the line. It was obvious that the officer was angry as he took the phone from the distraught woman and explained to the father that he needed to come to the hospital. He didn't even let the man know that the child was still alive! Snatching the phone before the man hung up, Jeremy told David that she was still alive and that it was Kara, but his own anger got the best of him when he asked the man if he had hit Savannah. Though David apologized for his actions, Jeremy stared at his mother's injured face. It was just not enough to say he was sorry. Of course he had to forgive the man, but he had full intentions of protecting his mother at any cost.

After David hung up, Jeremy called his supervisor at his new job. He was still in the probationary period, but this was important. Though his boss was less than sympathetic concerning his sister's accident and the need for his presence at the hospital, the boy insisted that he could not come in.

....

The soothing hand of an old woman lit on David's shoulder. David wondered how long he slept in the grass, unable to shake his despair and the groanings in his spirit to meet the task at hand. The soft voice of Maria Scallion filled his ears, though he was still unable to look up. "David," sounded the urgent utterance. "Savannah is on the phone. Seems she went to her son Jeremy's apartment. The police have been looking for you both for hours." David's heart sank even more, reaching a depth of mental anguish he never knew existed. Kara! It had to be Kara! Images of the accident scene he passed on the way flashed through his mind. He pushed back the rising panic within him just enough to rise to his feet and make those endless steps to the house.

What would he say to Savannah? Swallowing hard, David reached for the phone. "Savannah?" he squeaked. "Is that you?"

The voice on the other end was incomprehensible. It was followed by another voice, a strong male speaking. "This is Sergeant Merdail of the Glendale police. We need for you to come and identify your daughter. She has been in an accident and has no identification on her. Please be at Mercy Hospital as soon as you can, but drive safely. Do you understand?" Though the sergeant was seething with anger, he maintained a professional demeanor. The marks on Savannah's face had given him no points with the authorities, though they had no proof of their origins.

"Yes sir," he gasped, nearly dropping the phone. As he was about to hang up, he heard someone else speaking.

"Wait, David! Don't hang up yet! This is Jeremy. Mom is too hysterical to identify her, but it is Kara. She's not dead like they made it sound, at least not yet! But she's not conscious either. They don't think she is going to make it. It was real bad. The other kids in the car are all dead. I think they were drinking. We gotta pray! Please don't give up! Mom needs us." He hesitated. "Sorry, sir, but I gotta ask. Did you hit my mom? She looks awful!" David started to cry again. This young boy he had so severely judged was taking far better care of Savannah than he was. "Did you hit my mom?" the voice insisted.

"Yes, son, I did. I lost my temper." He paused. "Honestly, it has never happened before, and by God's grace it will never happen again. Please tell her I'm sorry. Please hold her for me. And forgive me for judging you."

"I forgive you," the boy responded with hesitant determination. "But it really can't happen again. I'll do anything to stop you, even if it means sending you to jail. I've been cheated out of my mom all my life, and no one will ever take her from me again. I am going to ask her to move in with me!" With this both men hung up the phone, and David wondered if he had lost Savannah forever.

David did not even remember the drive to the hospital. His mind seemed to be on auto-pilot. His entire existence had been reduced to a collection of crumbled debris, as if some giant creature had snatched it up and wadded its contents into a jumbled ball to discard it. Surely nothing could ever be right again. From the emergency room, security escorted him, a hodgepodge of trapped emotions, down a hall to identify his daughter.

Entering the room, David saw her. It was his Kara, lying in a broken mass of flesh and rescue equipment. In the bed next to her he saw Savannah, holding tightly to what remained of her child, sobbing uncontrollably. Then he saw the boy, a well kept blond youth, donning an oddly fierce but gentle expression.

David was totally disarmed by the young man's appearance. He was nothing like David had imagined. An air of confidence preceded the youth as he approached, held out his hand, and introduced himself. "I am Jeremy," he began, in a strange mixture of politeness and grim determination. "I am... I mean Savannah is my mother." Pausing after David's feeble handshake, he continued. "She hasn't let go of Kara since we arrived. No one has been able to pry her free. I guess they finally gave up, since they say it is only a matter of time till... you know... she dies," he whispered.

At this point, David could no longer control himself. He fell to the floor on his knees beside the bed, weeping. "I am so sorry, Savannah! Please forgive me! Please come back Kara! Please, God! Give us another chance! Don't take my baby! Please don't take our baby!" he wailed.

Savannah lifted a single finger off Kara's arm, slightly touching David, tucking one of his fingers beneath her hand, as if in a feeble attempt to comfort him. His lifeless limbs could not respond, however. David felt his body disconnect from his brain, and he could not move. Hospital staff grabbed the moment and pried

Savannah and David off the child. The couple watched helplessly as they whisked her, bed and all, to the intensive care unit, unwilling for the parents to follow. "I am so sorry, Savannah! I am so sorry!" wailed the bereaved father. He chanced one brief look into Savannah's face, her cheek and eye horribly blackened and swollen, and at that moment, he wanted to die.

....

Everything was black with no vision or movement until it started. It was that dream again. Kara was a little girl, holding that old Barbie doll. She was hiding in a dark closet, but she had to go to the bathroom. The music was deafening, possessing a strange shelter of anonymity, as the child stole down the hallway into the bathroom. There was a bit of vomit on the floor that she stepped over, but she made it to the toilet. Creeping quietly but swiftly back down the hall, the relieved little girl entered her room and reached for the closet door. That nasty odor again filled the child's nostrils, and before she could scream, the man's disgusting hand was over her mouth. She felt like she would vomit from the stench.

Suddenly Kara felt herself lifted out of the child's body, hovering in the room above her, a helpless witness to what was about to take place. The relief of not feeling the child's pain was overshadowed by the horror of the knowledge of what was about to transpire. The little girl was not Kara at all, though she looked much like her. Kara witnessed the terrible attack as the man stripped the child and violently raped her, slapping her repeatedly as she tried to scream. Each penetration resulted in massive amounts of blood, as the little girl was bleeding profusely, struggling under the beast who held her in his grasp.

It seemed to go on and on, like it would never stop. He only paused occasionally to curse at her for fighting him and to slap her again. Kara heard words she had never heard before and witnessed a brutality beyond her imagination. Still she could not wake up. When he finally stopped, the man growled at the child who was lying in her own blood. "You clean that up, and do it now! You tell anyone, and you are dead!" Then looking back over his shoulder, he sneered, "Happy Birthday, Savannah! Happy Birthday!" At this, the monster left the room.

Kara still struggled to wake up with no avail. Could this really be That Woman? Somehow that title did not fit so well anymore. Is this what these dreams had all been about? A sick feeling settled upon her as she tried to make sense of it all. The child, however, unaware of her observer, struggled to her feet, still crying. She made feeble attempts to obey the voice and clean up the blood on the floor, collapsing occasionally. She's hurt, Kara thought. Why doesn't she go get her mother? Instead the little girl struggled through the cleanup, still bleeding, until she curled up on a cot in the corner, again clutching her doll and sucking her thumb, and fell asleep.

Kara was again enveloped by the darkness. Unable to wake up, yet unable to fully sleep, she decided that she was still in the dream. Her mind was reeling with unanswered questions and emotions. What was taking place? Gradually, she saw a faint light fill the space as she found herself still overlooking the little girl. A rather unkempt woman entered the room. She looked very much like That Woman with a lot of makeup on, wearing a very short dress with a plunging neckline. Her face was heavily made up. This was actually That Woman, Kara decided, rather than the little girl. But when she peered closer, the woman had much darker hair and piercing blue eyes. As she opened her mouth, this creature seemed to have a more hardened carriage about her. As much as it would be more comfortable to imagine this woman as the whore who had given away Kara's brother and killed her sister, fitting to her accusations towards Savannah, this woman was not her at all. It dawned on Kara that this was the child's mother.

"Get up!" barked the woman. "You can't miss the bus to school or they will be calling here!" As the child lifted her head, her mother gasped. There were several bruises on her face and over her body, and she lay in a pool of blood. "What happened?" snapped the woman. "Who were you with last night?" The voice sounded more like a scolding than that of a concerned parent. When the child did not answer, she demanded again, "Who was it?"

"Uh… Uncle… J… Jimmy," whimpered the stammering child, still crouched in the corner.

"Don't you ever say that again!" screamed the woman. "Uncle Jimmy lets us live here! You aren't going to send my only brother to jail! You always wear those tight shirts! You did this!" The woman left the room and quickly returned with a t-shirt much too big for the child. "Wear this! It's all we got!" At that the woman threw the shirt at the cot, cursing at the child, and stormed from the room.

The child struggled to get dressed, putting on a pair of green stretch pants and the pink shirt she was given, along with a pair of weather beaten socks and old white tennis shoes. As she barely finished, her mother returned. The child was yanked off the bed and dragged into the bathroom, where her mother liberally and quite roughly applied her makeup to the little girl's face, covering the marks from the night before. She also covered a few visible areas on her neck, arms, and legs. "Don't wash this off till you get home!" she ordered. "And under no circumstances are you to go into the nurse's office! Do you understand?" The child nodded. "You disobey me, and I will beat you myself!" Satisfied that the worst bruises were covered by clothing, she pushed the child out the door towards the bus stop, offering one last look of warning.

Kara tried to push back a thought that began to creep into her mind. Savannah never wore makeup and had been resistant to Kara's desire to use it, which of course encouraged Kara to apply it all the more liberally. Wanting to remain angry with That Woman who had given her brother away, who had murdered her sister, she stuffed the idea not very successfully into the back of her consciousness. Why couldn't she wake up? It was as if she was watching a horror movie from which she could not escape. She had never seen a movie this vivid, yet these visions were inescapable. She could not even turn her head to look away. Kara saw the little girl, wearing an excessive amount of makeup, a loose pink shirt, pale green slacks, and old tennis shoes walk a bit painfully up the steps onto the school bus and sit in a lone seat, as the bus drove away. The fear in the child's eyes was penciled into her memory permanently.

Kara stayed behind, watching the mother go back into the old shack. In a kitchen scattered with empty alcohol bottles, some sprinkled white powder, and a few syringes with uncovered needles attached, the assailant sat calmly at the table, sipping a cup of muddy appearing coffee. "You get the little liar off to school?' the man snarled. "Got a mind to give her a good beating myself, her lying like that. She probably found one of your guys last night and got in over her head!"

"Be careful, Jimmy! We could both go to jail if anyone sees those bruises. I'd keep her home, but with all the school she's missed, they are likely to send out truant officers or a social worker or something! Keep your hands off her! I can't believe you couldn't even do it without all those marks!"

"So you believe her? You could be out on the streets again if you keep it up!" he snarled. He pushed the black matted locks from his face and continued to sip on his coffee.

"You get enough money out of me! These men pay you pretty well!" she bantered back, storming from the room. "I'm going to take a nap! This is Friday. It should be a busy night!"

"More than you're worth, that's for sure," he retorted.

Everything went black, and Kara again struggled to wake up to no avail. Would this night ever end? Though relieved that the images seemed to be gone, Kara's mind was swirling with questions. What was all this about? Why did she have to see all this awful stuff? She felt sickened by the sights, unable to cast them away. Where was she anyway? Where had she fallen asleep? Kara began to remember the note she had written. Was she asleep in the car?

Images again began to surface. She was the little girl again, hiding in a closet. She felt absolutely terrified as the voices from the other room floated into her ears. The music was loud again, and someone was arguing down the hall. Kara struggled desperately to separate again from the child, but she could not accomplish it. Reaching under the big pink shirt, her hand stroked her belly, which had become tight, large, and rounded. She felt puzzled and afraid, not understanding what sickness this was that seemed to be making her so fat. At times, her whole stomach moved. Her Barbie doll lay beside her.

Horrified, Kara frantically struggled again until she was finally free of the child, looking down on her. At that moment, the child's mother entered, opened the closet door, and grabbed the child from her hiding place. The woman gasped as she saw the belly the child had been stroking. "What have you done?" she shrieked. "Just when were you planning to tell me?" With this, she slapped the child across the face. The child looked confused. Pulling the child's shirt down and yanking her to her feet, the woman walked brusquely down the hall, child in tow. "Jimmy?!" she yelled. "Jimmy!" She walked up to the man, and Kara could again smell the sweat, alcohol, vomit, and who knew what else that enveloped the man.

"You gotta call someone now! This little brat is pregnant! And don't tell me you don't have the money! If she blames it on you, you'll be in jail!"

"I'll take care of it," he grumbled. "I have to take care of everything! Should just beat it out of her! Next time watch her closer around your friends!"

"Just do it!" she snarled. "I am not raising another brat anyway! Got no time for that!"

"You ought to just sell it," he mumbled.

"She's got to go to school, you idiot!"

"You better never call me that again! Brother or not, you work for me! I don't put up with that from any of my girls!" With that he swiped her across the face with his open hand. Seeing the child wince at the sight, he struck her as well, slapping her in the chest to avoid bruising her face. Looking at the little girl and her mother, the man shouted, "Get in the car! We will take care of this right now!"

The man grabbed a stack of bills from a drawer and stuffed them into his pocket. Kara watched as the child was pushed into a car by her mother and uncle. What could the man possibly have in mind? It seemed they drove for hours, and it had become dark. They made their way onto some back country roads, so the ride was bumpy. The car finally stopped in front of an old barn. "Just stay here!" he demanded over his shoulder. Jimmy walked up to the house near the barn and knocked on the door. Kara could see him talking to a short, stocky man with long graying black hair. The man went inside the house briefly, returning with a black bag, which he took into the barn.

Dread settled over Kara's thoughts as she contemplated what these men must have in mind. Were they going to kill the little girl? Why did she have to watch this? Jimmy and the child's mother pulled her from the car. Terror overtook the child's countenance as they led her unwillingly into the barn. The man with the bag turned on a dim light as they entered. "Want any pain medicine for the little girl?" the stranger asked. "It costs extra."

"No." Jimmy's answer was abrupt. "But you better put a gag in her mouth. This one can scream pretty loud." The child's mother glared at him. It was obvious he had heard her scream before, not that she really had any doubt.

Kara wanted to look away as they placed the gag in the child's mouth, but she could not. She seemed to be a slave to the nightmare. They tied the little girl to a thin bed that appeared like a gurney, and Kara observed the ghastly details that followed. Removing the child's panties and spreading the child's legs painfully apart, the stranger shoved an instrument inside her. She tried to pull away, crying behind the gag. "Why'd you wait so long?" he grumbled. "She must be at least seven months pregnant!"

The child struggled so much that the stranger seemed to be having trouble with what he was trying to do. Her screams were muffled but audible behind the gag, and Jimmy slapped her across the face. Reaching up inside her, the man seemed to be pulling something out. Sweat was running down the child's face, and she appeared to be in absolute agony. To Kara's horror, the man retracted his arm from inside the girl, holding a baby. It was a little girl, and as it struggled to breath, the stranger placed his hand over its face, suffocating it. The child looked on, still crying and trying to scream behind her gag. She could not struggle free. The man threw the dead baby into an old bucket, along with the other bloody contents.

Blood was everywhere. "I gotta give her something. She has to stay still so I can sew her up!" When Jimmy tried to protest, the stranger snarled. "I am not going to jail for you! This little girl could die!" He pulled out a large syringe and needle and gave her a shot. The child's mother stared at the needle as he inserted it into the child with a kind of hungry look, like she wanted it for herself. The child's mother mumbled something about it being a waste. After the little girl lost consciousness, the stranger continued his work. When he finished, he untied the sleeping child and carried her to the car, where she instinctively curled up in a ball, reached for her doll, placed her thumb in her mouth, and continued her sleep.

Kara was shocked into numbness as she again became enveloped by the darkness. Was the little girl really her mother? Why did she have to watch this? Horror and rage enveloped her as she contemplated this sight. Had she really just witnessed the murder of her sister? This just could not be! Kara shoved the thoughts again into the blackness that had so recently become her friend. Though she could not wake up, she was now enveloped by a total lack of thoughts and dreams.

Chapter 4

Savannah opened her eyes to look across the bed at the body of her lifeless daughter. Her eyes stung and were swollen from crying. The only movement Kara made was the forced respirations of the machines to which she was attached. How had life evolved into this? Did God even care about her private Hell? David had gone home to sleep, knowing he had to keep things together to work. Kara had been in this state for several months now, and people were beginning to insist that continuing this kind of care for the child was both useless and exorbitantly expensive. Savannah refused to leave the child's side, though she frequently overheard the mumbled expressions of disapproval from those around her. David tried to be supportive, but he was dealing with his own grief. Though the couple had reconciled, his response was to further bury himself in his work.

The room had grown dark, with only the occasional flickering of lights from the medical equipment. Nursing staff did their best to keep the door closed so Savannah could rest, but the sporadic beeping of the apparatus attached to Kara's body could not always be silenced. If only Kara would wake up. David had been very patient, but money was running out to continue this care, and the insurance company was threatening not to pay.

Savannah barely closed her eyes again when she heard a rustling behind her. The door had not opened, and she could not imagine who could be in the room, but she was too tired and emotionally drained to even bother turning her head. Instead, she lay motionless beside her daughter.

The room was filled with a soft light as she heard His Voice. "Savannah?" Her heart ached, knowing His Voice but feeling too hurt and betrayed to answer. She knew she could not hide the anger that was growing within her. He knew everything. She was so enveloped in her sadness that she barely considered the rarity of this opportunity, with her Lord speaking so clearly to her. "Savannah," He proceeded softly, "would you like to crawl up onto My lap?" At this, she began sobbing uncontrollably. Though she did not move, she knew she was instantly in His arms, in His embrace. The tears flowed in an eternal torrent, as she lay in His arms, swaying as a little child cradled in a rocking chair. Neither said a word as He simply rocked her ceaselessly for what seemed like hours. Visions and memories of her past paraded before her, every sadness she had ever encountered, as He stroked her and comforted her. She saw the rape, she saw the abortion, she remembered her uncle's yearly visits to her on her thirteenth, fourteenth, and fifteenth birthdays to attack and torment her again. It was always "Happy Birthday, Savannah" with threats that kept her from crying out as she had the first time. She had known there was no one to come to her rescue anyway. She felt a sense of satisfaction on her sixteenth birthday when she sneaked away with a boy she met at school, Jeremy's father. At least this time she was with someone she wanted to be with. How he had captured her favor! But he exited her life after she hid with him for those eleven short months. Visions of the beating floated through her mind after she refused the abortion. The strikes from that belt hurt as though it was but a moment ago. She remembered sneaking to the orphanage to give Jeremy away. Savannah remembered talking with her mother, who was in the hospital from an overdose, just before she died. Her mother begged her for forgiveness, and though she told her she forgave her, she never really let it go. How dare she ask that at the very end of her life! She remembered begging on the streets and hiding in deserted buildings to stay away from Jimmy. She remembered so many things!

Savannah looked down at her hands where she felt she was clutching something. It was her old Barbie doll! As she looked up, she could only see His large arms engulfing her, as if she were an infant compared to Him. She felt His heartbeat, which seemed as if it would break. In that instant, she released her pain into Him and relaxed. She remembered the Scallions. She remembered getting saved, meeting David, getting married, being really happy for the first time in her life, having Kara without fear of someone taking her away.

Savannah looked again at the doll. Instead of the old Barbie, she saw a brand new one. On closer observation, the doll was an exact replica of Kara. A mixture of emotions filled her being as she realized what the Savior was telling her. "Savannah," He began. "I gave you Kara. She was given for your healing, but you have chosen to live your life through her. You have made her your little doll. You have tried to make her everything you were not. She can not be Kara and you at the same time. You need to let her go. Give her back to Me."

Savannah was filled with horror. Why must He take Kara away? The torrent of tears resumed in full fury. She wanted her child back so profoundly. For the first time in her Christian walk, Savannah pulled herself out of her Savior's arms. She refused His comfort. The words of Jesus echoed in her mind. "He who loves father or mother more than Me is not worthy of Me. And he who loves son or daughter more than Me is not worthy of Me." Matthew 10:37 (NKJV). A coldness rested over Savannah's heart as she slipped into the bed beside Kara into a fitful sleep.

....

From the blackness, Kara's dreams began again. She was now a young girl, and it was her sixteenth birthday. A young man looking incredibly like Jeremy was with her, holding her hand. "Come with me," he coaxed. Everything in her fluttered with excitement. She wanted to be with this boy with the blazing blue eyes and blond hair. Kara was painfully aware of her own unkempt appearance. She was wearing no makeup, and though she was fairly clean, her clothes left much to be desired. Seeming to sense her dilemma, the boy escorted her to a clothing store, where he bought her two new outfits. "It's your birthday present," he said. She was completely taken by him. The boy then escorted her to a school, where she went into the office and informed the people there that she was quitting high school. No one seemed to care. She sneaked into the gym showers and cleaned up, putting on one of the new pieces of clothing, and returned to where the boy waited.

"Wow!" exclaimed the boy. "You look incredible!"

The two walked hand in hand until they came to a small one bedroom apartment, which they entered. "We can stay here now," he continued. "My parents are paying the rent till I get a job. Sort of a graduation present since they thought they'd never get me through high school," he laughed. His laughter had a healing quality. The vision vanished, with Kara a bit angry to see it go. This was a happier dream, and she did not want it to stop.

The dream resumed with a pregnant Kara, trying to tidy up a now very cluttered and dirty apartment. The boy was there, but he sounded angry. "You can't live here anymore!" he shouted. "I don't need a baby, and I am too young to be stuck with one girl anyway! You don't know how to clean, your cooking is terrible, and I just can't do this! You are due to have this baby in another month, and I am not ready for that! I am taking you home!"

Terror filled Kara's heart as she realized where the boy would take her. She was eight months pregnant and returning home to a nightmare! She wanted to run but could think of no where to go. A not so gentle hand grabbed her arm, escorting her back to her dungeon. The boy knocked on the door and quickly took off before anyone answered. Greeted at the door by a chilly woman who asked why she bothered to come home, Kara was relieved that the loose shirt successfully covered her condition. The woman was so strung out on drugs that she paid no attention to the girl's appearance anyway. But Kara could not escape attention for long. About a month later, a slightly older looking Jimmy decided he had been cheated out of his last birthday visit, and he came in to Kara's room. She realized at this point that this had been a yearly ritual. As his filthy hands stripped off her clothes, he saw the now nine month pregnant girl. Angrily, he pulled her shirt back over her and dragged her instead to see the woman in the other room.

"Guess your little brat was busy while she was gone!" he yelled, lifting her shirt. "Just who's supposed to pay for this one?" Then he dragged her to the car, throwing her in, her mother behind. Kara was in shock. Were they really considering trying to force her to have another abortion at this late date? Kara cried and screamed all the way to the old barn that she remembered from the other nightmare. Jimmy slapped her and told her to shut up, but she persisted. The woman hit her, too, keeping her from her frequent attempts to open the car door. Arriving at the old barn, Jimmy got out. He reached around and punched the girl in the mouth, screaming at her to shut up. The woman kept her restrained while Jimmy went to the man's door, and the pair dragged her into the barn. When they brought her to the abortionist, however, she fought him with such fierceness that he refused to complete the task. "I can't work like this! Get her out of here!" he yelled. "Why did you wait so long again?"

The woman and uncle were absolutely furious. Grabbing her by the hair, they threw her again into the car, the woman screaming that they had no room for a baby, and that if she insisted on having this one, it would be sold on the black market for drugs. This creature seemed to take some pleasure in that thought and appeared to calm down.

Back in their shack, the woman resumed her tirade. She dragged Kara, accompanied by the uncle, to a back room. He turned up the music real loud, Kara was stripped, and the woman began to beat her with a belt. Kara struggled from within the child, barely becoming free before the strap landed for the second time on the girl's bare skin. The uncle watched smugly, smirking as if being entertained.

Kara was again looking on from above the teen, as the woman continued to beat her endlessly, until it seemed she had released all the rage of her own life on the victim, who lay sobbing in the corner. Kara caught her own breath as she witnessed a few of the blows landing on the girl's pregnant belly, which she had tried to protect with her arms. After the woman left the room, the girl's uncle sneered at her and placed his hands all over her body. He aimed a kick at her belly, but the alcohol in his system caused him to miss, his shoe landing on her thigh instead. Angry at his own clumsiness, he slapped her across the face and growled, "I'll be back for you later! You just better not move! You still owe me for your last birthday! It's pretty cheap payment for staying here all these years." Kara overlooked the scene in horror, understanding that the man's drunkenness was the only thing that delayed his plan to rape the girl again despite her pregnant state. He closed and locked the

83

door and walked away. Kara watched, unable to turn away, as the girl waited until no one was looking and grabbing her clothes and a makeup bag, she squeezed out through a window. Hurrying away, she walked for a long while until she came to the door of the apartment where the baby's father lived, knocking. As she cried, telling him she had no where else to go, the boy simply told her he could not care for a baby and that this was her problem. She should have taken protective measures to keep from getting pregnant in the first place. He didn't seem to even notice the marks on her body from the beating, though she had a bright red welt where the belt had landed on her face, and her lip was bleeding.

The girl started walking again, pausing to take a breath between the rapidly progressing labor pains, until she came upon an old, deserted business building. The windows were all broken, providing easy entry. Inside, she found an old blanket and lay on it, struggling in her pain. The girl's water broke, spreading fluid everywhere. Kara watched as the girl fumbled through the agonizing process of delivering her baby alone. It seemed to take several hours. Cleaning him up as best she could, she wrapped him in the blanket on which she had been laying and began walking again. She walked for a long while, occasionally looking at the baby and stroking his face, crying. The girl smiled at him through her tears, hugging him close to her body. She stopped momentarily to catch her breath, then hurried on. The girl seemed to know exactly where she was going.

Ahead, Kara saw a large, brick building. The name on it was simply "Westside Orphanage". The girl walked up a set of stairs, a seemingly agonizing task that took some time, sobbing uncontrollably. Entering the old stark building, she walked up to the first person she saw, thrusting the baby into a lady's arms, and said, "Please take care of my baby. I can't take care of him." She paused. "His name is Jeremy. If he wants to know who I am when he grows up, my name is Savannah McNeill." Before anyone could ask any more questions, she darted away.

The girl was returning to the shack where her abusers lived, still sobbing. Why was she going back? Arriving at the house, there were police everywhere. Kara sensed the girl had an extreme fear of the police, observing as she stayed at a distance. Next to the police cars sat an ambulance, and she watched as paramedics took the woman who must have been the girl's mother out on a gurney. Several male visitors were being removed in handcuffs, and the girl seemed at a loss for what had just happened. Her seventeenth birthday was just one week away.

After everything died down, the girl approached a nearby neighbor to find out what had just taken place, taking care not to reveal the injured side of her face. "A drug bust in that old whore house," someone said, barely looking at her in the dark. "Think the lady overdosed on drugs and was taken to the hospital. Bet her brother, the pimp, got away. They won't get anything on him. He's too slick for that. Some people think she has a daughter, but I really don't know. I've never seen her anyway, and I've lived here a long time. There used to be a kid that got on the bus here, but no one has seen her for quite a while either. If she did have a daughter, I'm sure she is long gone." The girl began walking away, seemingly not to be recognized, until she came to the old building where she delivered her child. She looked faint as she went in and lay on the floor, falling fast asleep. She seemed to be gasping for air.

Kara looked on helplessly, unable to free herself of this ordeal. It was dark, and the air held the smell of mildew mixed with blood. The girl was breathing heavily. Startled by a loud noise from outside, the girl was alert again. She forced herself into an upright position, exited the building, and started walking.

Kara saw a hospital up ahead and wondered if the girl had decided to get care. She seemed to be headed straight for it. As she entered the emergency room doors, however, Kara was astonished. She simply slipped into a bathroom to clean up and covered her wounds with a lot of old makeup foundation she carried, and she proceeded to the counter to ask for the room number of a woman Kara instinctively knew was the girl's mother. It seemed obvious that the girl had learned well the best use for makeup, and it was odd that she would be so used to carrying it. The man at the desk quoted a room number, stating she could not have visitors in the intensive care unit unless it was family. "Are you related?" he asked. Kara felt the girl hesitate as she stated that the woman was her mother. The man then called someone, who escorted her to the woman's bedside.

The woman was unconscious with tubes coming out from nearly every bodily orifice. Machines flickered with light and sound, attached to the woman's frame. The teen held her hand. Why did she even care about this creature who had so long been her tormenter? The girl just sat at her side until she fell asleep beside her oppressor.

Nurses were busy everywhere. A particularly heavy set lady with short black hair and dark brown eyes, looking to stand barely five feet tall, was caring for the woman. She heard the woman talking to coworkers. "She might make it for a bit, but her kidneys are shutting down. Even if we bring her back, I doubt she'll make it for long. Just too much damage. Why do these people do this? If they want to kill themselves, they should do it right. This will be another one at the tax payers' expense. Wonder what will happen to the girl."

Another continued, "Think there's a brother somewhere. Maybe she can live with him. Maybe she just lives on the streets anyway." Kara was angered at their coldness. Couldn't they see that these were real people they were talking about? She thought that if they had tried at all, they would have seen the wounds that were still visible through the makeup. At this point, Kara was again enveloped in darkness.

Kara's dream resumed a bit later. She sensed that it was the girl's birthday. The girl was still sitting beside the woman in the hospital. The woman looked terrible. Her skin color was yellow, and her breathing was sporadic. Suddenly the woman seemed to force herself awake. "Savannah," she began. Startled, the girl looked up. "I'm sorry," she whispered. "My life was so miserable that I ruined yours too. Will you forgive me? Please?" Kara was aghast as the girl nodded. How could this woman even begin to deserve this? "Uncle

Jimmy is your guardian now. I'm not gonna make it, Savannah. You gotta do what he says, child, or you won't have a place to stay. He'll be looking for another girl. You better just suck it up and do what he says." The girl was emphatically shaking her head no.

"I can't, Mama. I can't! Don't die! Please!" she sobbed as the woman closed her eyes and stopped breathing. As the medical staff flooded the room, the girl faded into the dark corners of the room where no one could see her and bolted out of the hospital, disappearing into the streets.

Everything went dark for Kara again. Why wasn't she waking up? It seemed like she had been asleep for a long time. Struggling to regain her memory, she recalled being in the backseat with Daniel. His rapid advance had disgusted her, and she had fought him off. Was he actually planning to rape her? But what had happened after that? Kara was filled with dread as new thoughts invaded her mind. The memory of a deafening crash and a mass of confusion entered her consciousness. Was she dead?

....

David unlocked the door to the house. He was home from work. No one else was there, and he knew Savannah was still at the hospital. As he lifted the cover of the mailbox, he pulled out a letter and opened it, walking into the house. Pulling a pair of reading glasses from a nearby coffee table, he proceeded to read the letter. David's sadness was deepened into dread as he studied the words before him. The insurance company had sent a letter, stating that he had only one appeal left concerning their payment of Kara's care. She had been in a coma for over eight weeks now with no improvement, and unless he consented to brain studies to determine the viability of the child, all payments would be discontinued. If brain studies showed little or no activity, they would no longer cover rescue care. He had five days to respond.

David no longer cared that there would be no supper ready for him tonight. He couldn't eat anyway. When would this hell be over? He knew Savannah would never let go of Kara, and he was sure that if he consented to turning off the machines, it would be the end of their marriage. He had already caused so much damage from the judgments he had made about his wife with his pieces of information. Savannah had never spoken a word about the night he struck her, after she told him she had forgiven him. But things still didn't seem as they were before. She nearly winced whenever he passed her too quickly now, sending spears of regret throughout his being. In a way he felt this was unreasonable. Why hadn't she found a way to tell him about her background? If he had known the details, of course he wouldn't have blamed her. It also bothered him to know that there were probably many other pains she hadn't told him about. This seemed unfair, as he was left to wonder what else might surface.

David lay on the bed, overwhelmed with grief and confusion. "What am I supposed to do, God? Is Kara going to get better or not? It seems impossible, and Savannah won't let her go! I don't have the money for this if the insurance refuses to pay. Savannah will hate the brain studies, but I don't think I have a choice!" It was the first prayer he had uttered in over six months. David was so intensely exhausted from the entire ordeal that he fell asleep.

The room was dark, and he began to dream. It started with a nightmare. Someone was pulling his child from him, attacking her, while he could do nothing. Savannah was there, laughing at him, taunting his inability to rescue Kara. David groped in the darkness to find Kara again. He became angry as Savannah kept getting in his way. Anger became rage as he began viciously beating Savannah, and in an instant, he discovered it was Kara he was hitting. She was bleeding and running from him, as he pursued her, apologizing that he didn't know it was her.

David shook himself awake. What a tormenting nightmare! As he lay back against the pillow, a bright light entered the room. He felt a sense of awe mixed with terror as he recognized this presence. It was God again, and he was still reeling from the last encounter.

There was no face to be seen, only a Voice. "David" echoed the sound.

Swallowing hard, he answered, "Yes, Lord?"

"Why are you afraid?" He continued, much more gently than David expected. "Don't you know that I love you?"

David began to cry. He really had not believed that God loved him until now, especially in light of recent events. The thought overwhelmed him.

"It was just a bad dream, David, sent from the evil one to torment you and to put division between you and Savannah. Have you forgiven Savannah?"

"Yes, Lord. It wasn't even her fault. I forgave her."

"That is what misinformation and isolated facts do. You need to seek out the truth of a matter. But My forgiveness is much more than that, David. What if she had aborted a child before she met you? Would you love her less? And what if she was filled with too much sorrow to tell you about it? Could you forgive her then?"

David hesitated. "I don't know," he honestly replied. "I really don't know."

"I forgave all your sins with full knowledge of what you had done against me. I have forgiven Savannah. Whether or not you ever know all of her background, you must forgive her like that. Because you have not, you struggle to believe that I have forgiven you for hitting Savannah. She has forgiven you, though your hand still holds a stinging memory for her that will take much time to heal. It reminds her of times she has been hit before."

"But why can't she tell me all that stuff? Why did she have to hide it?"

"I saw a little boy, twelve, at school. He sneaked behind a building to kiss a little girl. The boy was horrified when the girl lifted up her dress in front of him, and she was wearing no undergarments. He ran back to play with his other friends, feeling completely embarrassed by what had taken place. Who have you told about that, David?"

He still shuddered at the memory, recalling his own sense of shame. Though logic would argue that he was innocent as he had not solicited the girl's behavior, the humiliation remained undiminished. He also knew that he was not supposed to be kissing a girl behind a building on a playground in the first place, and thus he had put himself in that vulnerable position. "No one," he answered.

"Savannah's memories are much more painful than that, David. 'Judge not, and ye shall not be judged: condemn not, and ye shall not be condemned: forgive, and ye shall be forgiven:' (Luke 6:37 KJV). Do you want to be forced to share all of your memories?"

"No," he replied. "I forgive her completely, no matter what."

It felt like God smiled. David even sensed the Father's arms around him as He continued. "David, you don't need to be so far away from Me. I have been with you for such a long while, but only you can decide to accept My nearness. You can learn that from Savannah." The man wept for what seemed a long while.

Mustering his voice again, David continued. "What about Savannah? She can't let go of Kara. Where do I go from here? Are you taking Kara from us?"

"All that will be revealed in time. There are still lessons to be learned, including trusting Me even when things are not as you want them to be. Knowing in your mind that you should trust me is not enough. You have to live it through your actions. You must believe that what I do is for your good, for Savannah's good, and for Kara's well being. Did you not give Kara to me when she was born?"

David gulped. "Yes, Lord, we did."

"Then if she goes home with me, how have I taken her? She is Mine."

The man became again a mass of tears, as he cried in his Savior's arms. He did not want to let Kara go, but she really was not his anyway. It seemed more than he could bear, even amidst God's comforting embrace.

"David," continued Father, "don't be afraid to do the brain studies. I will deal with Savannah. This has to be done." Sobbing uncontrollably, he found himself asleep with the words of Jesus echoing within him. "And ye have forgotten the exhortation which speaketh unto you as unto children, My son, despise not thou the chastening of the Lord, nor faint when thou art rebuked of him: For whom the Lord loveth he chasteneth, and scourgeth every son whom he receiveth. If ye endure chastening, God dealeth with you as with sons; for what son is he whom the father chasteneth not? But if ye be without chastisement, whereof all are partakers, then are ye bastards, and not sons." Hebrews 12:5-8 (KJV)

The room was pitch black when David aroused himself. He had forgotten to turn on any lights at all. Fumbling for the bedside lamp, David again wondered if the experience was a dream. It was real, he decided, whether in the form of a dream or not. His pillow was soaked, and in the midst of his pain, there was an odd sense of comfort. The clock read two in the morning.

Getting out of bed, the man walked to the bathroom where he tidied up. He knew what he had to do. This was not going to be easy.

With every step to the car, the pain in his chest intensified. He had to sign the papers that he and his wife had refused up to this point. The drive was grueling, as he made his way to seal what seemed would be the doom of his family. Nearly running a red light in his distracted state, he made his way into the parking lot of the hospital and to the main entrance.

No one even bothered to stop him at the door. They all knew him by now. He approached the nurse's station and asked to speak with Kara's nurse. A tall blond girl walked up to him, and at this point, he stammered out that he was ready to sign papers for the brain studies. She seemed a bit relieved as she gathered them and obtained his shaky signature. "They will be done later today," she stated flatly, a coldness in her delivery. After he walked away, she mumbled under her breath, "It's about time!"

Walking into Kara's room, he saw Savannah curled around the small frame of his child. He had not been there for two weeks and was not sure how his wife would respond. "Savannah," he whispered. Savannah looked up at him, still clinging to the child, her face flooded with tears. She said nothing. "Savannah," he continued. "I signed the papers. We have to know."

Savannah's expression was one of anguish, mixed with fury and resentment. David had never seen her this way. It seemed that all the terrors of her life were now condensed into this moment, making David actually feel afraid. "I am sorry, Savannah. It had to be done. This is what God wants us to do."

"He can't have her!" The words were filled with a venom and pain unmatched by anything the man had witnessed before in his life. When he reached to comfort her, she recoiled instantly, clutching the child in her arms. "He can't have her!" she repeated.

"Savannah! Listen to what you are saying! We gave Kara to God when she was born. We promised to trust Him. She is not ours to hang onto. You have to let her go! Only God knows what is best for Kara, and He is telling us to let her go. If we fight Him, we are putting our own needs in front of Kara's needs." He paused, realizing the awful truth. "Savannah, Kara might not want to come back." Where had that come from?

At this, Savannah began wailing uncontrollably again, and David quietly left the room.

Chapter 5

A sense of dread was mounting in Kara's heart. She knew something was wrong now. Was she dead? She cried out in the blackness, "Where are you God? Am I dead? I am sorry for the things I have said and done. Is it too late? What are these things I have been seeing? Are You tormenting me? Is this a part of Hell, where you see all the things about how you messed up? Is this Your way of punishing me for the way I treated Savannah (she still wasn't quite ready to call her Mom)?" The torrent of questions startled the child, who began to think they were futile and would not be answered at all. Another nagging thought taunted her. What if there really was no God?

At this point a bright light filled Kara's world. "Kara." It was a strong, kind Voice. "Have you forgotten that you gave your life to Me? I love you, and I have been waiting for you to talk to Me." Kara relaxed a bit, but the inquiries continued to invade her being.

"What about all the things I have done, You know, in………"

"In your secret place?"

"Yes, Lord. You saw that?"

He chuckled. "I was there with you all the time. I saw you before you were born. Did you think you could get away from Me?"

A bit of embarrassment came upon Kara. "I really am sorry, Lord."

"I know. I forgave you long ago on the cross. I knew your pain, and I knew you were struggling. But I did not desert you just because you were having problems. You never stopped confessing Me, not really. Although you were embarrassed about Me in the car with Daniel. That hurt, you know, but I knew your heart."

His words resounded in her heart. "Therefore whoever confesses Me before men, him I will also confess before My Father who is in heaven. But whoever denies Me before men, him I will also deny before My Father who is in heaven." Matthew 10:32-33 (NKJV)

"I came close," she mumbled.

Kara then felt something entirely wonderful. The hand of Jesus, scars and all, reached out and took hers, lifting her out of the darkness. "I have much for you to see," He told her, "much for you to learn." His Voice seemed to ring like music, mixed with bells and rippling waters. It had a refreshing quality, cleansing every sting of darkness in its path. "There are many lessons for you to learn."

"Were those lessons, seeing Savannah's pain?" she asked.

He seemed saddened. "Savannah's pain? I need to show you something again."

Instantly the vision of Savannah being beaten filled the air. The sight was crushing as she screamed in agony with no one to help. Kara longed to turn away, but instead the scene became worse. The thrashing went on and on, and Kara soon began to see blood coming from the wounds. The weapon slowly transformed into cruel whips, cutting the flesh beyond recognition. Kara tried to cry out but could not form a sound. The smell of dirt and blood filled the air, and still the beating continued. "No! Please, no!" her voiceless heart screamed. Still the beating went on. As the body began to fall to the floor, with a turn of the head, she witnessed the face of the marred creature before her. To her horror, it was not the face of Savannah at all. It was Jesus, the One who now held her hand! He was bleeding, he was taking the beating! Amidst all this, Kara saw the reflection of Savannah's face in His Eye. She stared, dumbfounded, as the beating continued. As she looked into His Eyes, she could see the reflections of all the people she had ever known, and many more besides. Her heart felt wounded beyond comprehension, a piercing she felt would never go away. She saw her own reflection in those Eyes!

"Savannah's pain?" the Voice continued.

"I am sorry," Kara replied. "You suffered so much on the cross."

"On the cross?" He said sadly. "Do you still not understand?"

Again she saw Him beaten, while cackling voices swirled about Him. The aroma of death filled the air. Kara waited for His explanation. Instead His questioning continued, as she watched Him being punished beyond what her mind could take in.

"When was it hardest to experience Savannah's torment, Kara? Was it while you were her, inside her flesh, or was it when you were watching what was happening from outside her body?"

Kara hesitated. At least when she was in Savannah's body she could turn away. But the intensity of being a part of her was excruciating as well. As she continued to partake of the horror, she sensed it would not go away until this was settled. "I… I don't know," she whispered. "It hurts so much both ways."

"Kara, I feel it both ways at the same time. The cross is merely a summation of all the horror of the ages. Every time my children suffer, I am there. I both observe what I can not change because of the free will I have given mankind, and I experience the pain as I live within them. The evil one revels in this knowledge, finding gleefully that I suffer so when he hurts my children. He is actually striking out against Me when he does these things." He paused. "So if I can forgive men of what they have done, can you, who have not been tormented in like manner, not do the same? How is it that men can hold anything to another's account when I have suffered all, yet forgiven them?"

At this Kara's heart felt as though it had been smashed into a million pieces. She was cut to a depth she had never known existed. For a moment she was in Him, feeling His lashes from every side, and she knew His mourning over those who did not comprehend. Kara was unable to even cry out to stop the images that now burned eternally within her. She knew she would never be the same again.

The Hand then lifted Kara out of this place, cradling her in His eternal comfort. She felt the peace, knew His love, and rested in His arms. But she knew the mark of this moment would never expire. She had been introduced to the suffering of her Lord. Softly she whispered, "I love you, Mama, I forgive you. I am so sorry for how I treated you. Please forgive me too." Resting on the chest of Jesus, she went to sleep.

....

Savannah awoke to a soft light in the room again. Her entire being ached from the bursts of emotion and the growing pain she felt in refusing her Lord. She knew David was right, but it was so hard to let go. Quietly weeping, Savannah began in a pleading whisper. "I am sorry, Lord. I am so sorry. Please don't leave me."

"Savannah." His voice brought healing even in the mention of her name. "Savannah. Climb into My lap. We need to talk."

Savannah reached cautiously for Him, feeling like a little child about to get a spanking for her obstinacy. She hurt so much already, however, it seemed that any blow would be better than this. As she was enveloped by His love, all she could do was cry.

"We have been friends for a long time," He continued. "Would you withhold your daughter from Me? You once told Me that she was Mine. Can you take better care of her than I can? Or is it more important to you that she be with you than that she be happy and safe with Me?"

Sobbing bitterly, Savannah responded. "I am sorry, Lord. It is just so hard. It hurts so much. But if You want her, she is Yours. This hurts more than anything I have encountered in my entire life, worse than all the bad things that happened when I was a little girl, but I won't hold her back from Your love." Savannah felt His pleasure as she released the words, and she leaned against His chest, still crying. His hand touched her head and moved it towards Kara, and she saw the only movement from her daughter since all this had begun. "This is My gift to you, Savannah. Listen, and comfort yourself in what you hear."

As though talking in her sleep, these words slipped from Kara's mouth: "I love you, Mama, I forgive you. I am so sorry for how I treated you. Please forgive me too." Again the child was gone.

Savannah's cries were now a mixture of joy and sorrow, remorse and comfort. It was a cup she had not wanted to drink that brought peace along with the bitterness. "Please tell her that I love her and that I forgive her. Please," she entreated. She finally gave her consent; no matter what God decided, she would accept it.

She felt her Savior smile and stroke her face. "She knows, Savannah. She knows. I let her hear your words." Savannah fell asleep, still desperately crying, in His arms. More gently than any earthy father, He placed her in the bed beside the lifeless child and put a blanket over her. "I will never leave you," He whispered in her ear. Peace enveloped Savannah as she entered into His rest.

. . . .

Kara reached out eagerly for the hand of Jesus. She had learned to love His approach. A sweet fragrance more soothing than any earthly perfume preceded His Voice, more pure than any crystal waters. It was as if the tinkling of tiny, scattered jewels fell with every word. And how she loved to hear Him call her name! When He said her name, the whole of her existence seemed to tremble and melt. "Kara, are you ready for another lesson?"

"I love you, Jesus!" The words were so inadequate, yet they gushed from the child. "I would go anywhere with You!"

"Really, Kara? Even if it hurts? Learning brings much pain for those who have been touched by sin."

"But I have to go, don't I? I have to see what You want to show me. It's the only way I get to hear Your Voice." She still felt the aching from the last lesson, but she knew she must go on. He smiled gently as He held her close, and she sensed they were off again.

Kara's eyes lighted on a small room. Daniel was there, and she was with him. Daniel was laughing scornfully as he taunted her faith. She remembered this conversation. She remembered feeling that she had nothing to answer. Kara felt embarrassed to witness this with Him at her side. "It's just the weak people who get religion, Kara. Jesus is just a crutch! Strong guys like me don't need that stuff." She watched as the scene continued. "Come on, Kara. Come over here with me." She had walked slowly over and sat next to the boy when he reached over and kissed her. "Isn't that better than your religion?" he quipped. Before Kara could answer, he tried to pull her shirt off.

"Daniel! No!" she objected. "You know what I believe about that!"

"You know what? We're done! I have needs, and if you are going to be like this, I'll get someone else. I think you better go home."

Kara had left crying. Here it was, her breakup with Daniel. She had tried to hide her tears when she reached home, but Kara was sure her mother had seen them anyway, before she darted up to her room.

"Why are you showing me this?" she asked her Lord. The memory stung as if someone had slapped her with a force that stifled her very breath.

Instead of giving an answer, He asked another question. "Kara, is it a weakness to come to Me? Am I a crutch for the feeble mind?" Kara remained silent, unable to answer. The words permeated her thoughts, "And He said to me, 'My grace is sufficient for you, for My strength is made perfect in weakness.' Therefore most gladly I will rather boast in my infirmities, that the power of Christ may rest upon me." 2 Corinthians 12:9 (NKJV) He seemed to wait for her answer.

"Well, maybe," she started. "But I guess that is ok."

"It is true that the weak come to Me, and at some time in every person's existence, they have to face the fact that they are weak and I am strong. But it is not a weakness to come. It is the only true strength any individual truly has, to walk away from his own strength and to rely on Me."

"But God has chosen the foolish things of the world to put to shame the wise, and God has chosen the weak things of the world to put to shame the things which are mighty;" 1 Corinthians 1:27 (NKJV)

"Was it weakness that drove the disciples to choose death rather than to deny Me? Remember Paul's words, 'For I am not ashamed of the gospel of Christ, for it is the power of God to salvation for everyone who believes, for the Jew first and also for the Greek.'" Romans 1:16 (NKJV) "Are these weak words?"

Kara felt the pain in her chest again. She knew there had been times she had believed Daniel's line and that she had secretly wanted to give in to him. Did all lessons really have to hurt this much? She felt as though someone had taken a very harsh scouring pad and scrubbed her insides until she was raw. Without a sound, the tears flowed down her face. Though she was sure it would intensify her agony, she had to ask. "Why does it matter if I have sex before I get married? What is so wrong with it?"

Visions of Savannah at twelve again filled Kara's heart. She was seeing the rape again. She wanted to protest that this was different, but He stopped her, placing a single finger over her mouth for a moment. As she looked, she saw what appeared like a huge, thick cloud of black dust around the man, flecks of filth that entered inside the child and covered her without as well. Kara was so intrigued by what she observed that she barely felt the gnawing pain of watching this again. "What is that cloud?" she asked.

"Every speck of that cloud, each individual particle, is a part of the man, a part of his sin. His very living cells are passed to her. Can this child remove these specks from her when her attacker is done? He has planted in her something she will struggle with for a lifetime. That is why the sin he now commits is so hideous to me. He deposited his darkness into an innocent child, maiming her permanently with his sin. Come, I will show you more." Reluctantly, she held His Hand.

This time Kara saw Savannah with Jeremy's father. It was her sixteenth birthday, and she seemed to want to be with the man. Kara felt herself enter Savannah. But as he leaned over her, a massive multi-colored cloud of similar particles encompassed him. These particles were all over and entering into the girl. Particles from her became a part of him as well. As they entered, Kara felt like someone had spread a mist of fine, cutting glass, ripping into every part of her being and suffocating her as she tried to take a breath. Though Kara was removed from the girl's body, the massive amount of particles had encompassed her and entered into every part of her body.

"Can you find an instrument so small to remove each of these?" He asked. "There are millions of these tiny particles that have now become a part of you. Will you remove them one by one that you would be free of this torment? They looked beautiful enough, but they are still sin. No surgery can remove these. The two become one in their sin. I work their entire lives to heal them, and they do get some relief. I do an amazing job when there is repentance. But this is only completely gone when the girl's body dies. They remain a silent source of pain and suffering long after forgiveness has come."

"So if a girl has had sex with a boy, it's too late to change. What would be her advantage of not doing it again? Isn't the damage already done?"

"Each time she sins, this occurs again. And having multiple partners escalates the pain immeasurably. Once she has sinned like this, she can turn to Me. I will help her when the time for a pure union in My eyes begins. But she will carry some of the results throughout her life on Earth, though she is often not even aware of the source of the problems she encounters. This is true for the man and for the woman alike. She carries his sin within her, and he carries hers. It is with difficulty that they break the emotional bonds as well. They will experience difficulties in future relationships and must turn to Me to overcome these in the best ways possible. Increasing this by further sin is not only an affront to Me but unwise for her personally as well, as she multiplies her sorrow each time she continues in her sin."

The agony within Kara was growing, as each sharp piece lodged somewhere within her. Yet catching her breath, she continued. "What about when someone is married? Wouldn't it be the same?" She could barely speak, as it seemed that each speck had grown into something much bigger inside her.

Again she saw Savannah, this time with David. There was a holy hush in the room, and Kara realized that this was their wedding day. Kara barely noticed as the shards of sin left scattered within her melted away, she was so enthralled by the holiness of the moment. As David leaned over Savannah, the particles about him were red and white and seemed more like a gentle mist. Yes, this was somehow much different than before.

"When two people are in a union that I have blessed, they still become one. That is why it is so important to choose wisely, for a lifetime. But when this happens, I am present. A holy joining of hearts takes place, because this union is not of sin. Though the two will still have to deal with the other's sins to some degree, they are joining in My love; My redemptive blood covers them, and the particles of My holiness buffer this union that they not be poisoned by one another. That is why the particles are red and white, as the white are those things purified by My fire and the red particles are that which remains, covered by the blood of My sacrifice. This is the joining that I desire, and it is most holy in My sight. Though they will have suffering in this world, I cover them. This is a powerful union that the enemy wants to destroy, for if these two can agree on anything, great things can take place. 'Again I say to you that if two of you agree on earth concerning anything that they ask, it will be done for them by My Father in heaven.' Matthew 18:19 (NKJV)." Kara wept, partly at the beauty of the sight she had seen and partly at the thought of what she would have lost if she had given in to Daniel.

"Why is this sin such an especially hard sin to fight? What makes some sins harder to resist than others?" Kara asked.

"The greater the loss involved, the more the evil one increases his designs to use it to destroy you and to ruin My true purposes in you. Usually sins with temptations of this magnitude are related closely to something quite precious. There are natural designs that are in you for a purpose, and it is the hope of the evil one to pervert these. The creation of life itself and the pattern for the truest of fellowship is encompassed in these relationships. Also, the temptation is especially increased when an individual has broken the holy protection I have formed around him from birth, by having committed these acts before. Since the behavior is designed in such a way that it continues throughout the duration of the marriage relationship, which is to be a life time, once someone has committed this act, a natural law is set in motion. It was never created as a one time act. Thus the desire is increased, though it is now in a perverted state, making it much more difficult to resist the next time. It is necessary that a couple in the bounds of marriage have this desire one for another in order to solidify the union and to propagate the human race through reproduction. It was never designed, however, to be used as recreation outside of marriage. This desire strikes at the very core of human relationships. Man was created for fellowship, to love one another as I have loved each of you, and My enemy delights in destroying all that is encased in a human soul that fulfills this purpose. Sexual union is but one part of this, though it is quite integral in the relationship of marriage. If he can pollute this, immense problems are set in motion, as you have observed. The evil one thrives on the satisfaction he receives by observing the total confusion created as he twists the bonds of human fellowship into something quite unholy. It is his way of sneering at the Maker."

The shards had cut so deeply in the vision that though they were gone, she still felt raw, as if her very insides were scraped and cut by the particles. "Why does all this have to hurt so much?" she insisted.

"I paid a great price to redeem My people. Yet when they continue to sin, there is a consequence, a cost. I am not mocked. When you sow sin, there is a price to pay. Each little shard has to be removed, as a physician performing a surgery. It usually cuts into the tender areas on the way out. That is why you have so much suffering in this world. I am removing the things you have chosen to hang on to. The part of you still clinging to that sin is scarred due to your own resistance to Me, because sin is such a serious thing. It must be completely removed in order for you to spend eternity with Me. There are no exceptions. It would be so much easier if you let go of it yourselves. There is no painless way to remove it and not have it return. It must be destroyed at the roots, but when these roots have been allowed to grow, they wind deep into your being."

Thoughts of the many times she had chosen to sin, even as a Christian, thinking it was just a little thing, floated through Kara's mind. Overwhelmed, she began to cry again. As she mused that she spent so much time crying during these interactions, Jesus started to speak with her again. "The tears are healing you, washing many things away. You are still dealing with your willful sins. I am teaching you concerning the sins from which you have never repented. Though you may have mumbled a quick prayer occasionally, you refused to face your sin and to turn away from it."

He held her close as she sobbed bitterly at her own decisions, convinced that this torment would never end.

Kara could not understand why she continued to ask questions, knowing full well that what followed was usually filled with agony and regret, but she was compelled to go on. "What happened to the other kids in the car that night?" she asked. "Are they alright?"

"Some choices have eternal consequences. These solitary choices are actually a summation of many decisions. Rebellion has a price." He spoke gently.

Kara gasped in horror. "Did they die?"

"Yes, Kara, all five of them." He paused. "We will not discuss that now. Just know that I am just, and their fates are with Me."

Kara frightened herself with the anger rising up within her. Despite her fear, however, it had to come out. She could not bury it, and she knew He saw it anyway. "That's not fair! If You care about people, how can You let this happen? Did they go to Hell? Why can't I know what happened to them?" She paused. Her anger boiled. "And why did You let that man kill my sister? What about that?" She caught her breath. There was no satisfaction in this, yet she continued. "Did You forgive the woman who raised my mom just because she asked at the last minute of her life, after all the terrible things she had done? I know You did!" Rage poured from her in a torrent that she could not control, and part of her did not even want to stop it.

In an instant she was at the foot of the cross, hurling insults at her Lord. He was being beaten with her every word. Each accusation landed a fresh blow as she looked on. Intermittently, she felt the lashes in her own flesh. She was joined to Him, and the pain would not go away. Every word stung like a bullet of broken glass, and the beating seemed endless, filled with her own fury. She felt lash after lash cutting past her flesh into her very soul, until she cried out, "Please, Lord! I can't bear this! Forgive me!" and Kara was in His arms again.

"Kara," came the stern but kind Voice. "I do not want you to so easily forget again. The pain is to keep fresh in your memory the seriousness of these lessons. Though you think you have learned not to judge, you now stand in judgment over the God of the universe. Did I not show you how I suffer with My children, how I truly see all? If I judge, My judgment is true. But men have judged themselves unworthy of Me. They make their own choices. 'For God did not send His Son into the world to condemn the world, but that the world through Him might be saved. He who believes in Him is not condemned; but he who does not believe is condemned already, because he has not believed in the name of the only begotten Son of God. And this is the condemnation, that the light has come into the world, and men loved darkness rather than light, because their deeds were evil. For everyone practicing evil hates the light and does not come to the light, lest his deeds should be exposed.' John 3:17-20 (NKJV)" He paused. "Do you think it would have been kinder for your sister to have grown up as Savannah did? You think you suffer

111

from watching a baby killed. Yet I must look on every single time, observing as millions are murdered in My sight, watching as each baby is aborted, knowing the spirit and full potential of every little child that I breathed life into. Each screaming child, each life that is snuffed out, is fully known of Me. And you accuse Me? And are you angry because I forgave a dying woman who never knew love? It was your mother's love for her that led her to a place to ask for forgiveness. She turned to Me in the only way she knew how in the end. She still had to face her sin, even as you are doing now. Kara, as I told you, there are consequences for your sin. You felt My stripes because I want you to remember. Pain is the only thing that sinful man seems to respond to. I must bring correction lest you be destroyed in your own darkness. This is the mystery encompassed in the verses in Luke 12:47-48 (NKJV), 'And that servant who knew his master's will, and did not prepare himself or do according to his will, shall be beaten with many stripes. But he who did not know, yet committed things deserving of stripes, shall be beaten with few. For everyone to whom much is given, from him much will be required; and to whom much has been committed, of him they will ask the more.' You have been given much, and thus you are more responsible for your choices. This pain will remain in you for some time now, so that you do not choose this way again."

Kara could not speak. She wept uncontrollably as He held her close to His chest. She could hear His heart beat, and it felt as if His heart were breaking with hers as she drifted into sleep, the stinging of those lashes and His words now etched into her being, aching long after her rest began. "Rest for a while," He whispered. "Rest. There is still more to learn."

....

David heard the alarm echo throughout the empty house. Was it eight o'clock already? He had scheduled off work today to be at the hospital with Savannah while the tests were being done. He wondered if she would even talk to him. She had been so upset after he signed the papers. Still, he had to try. He was learning that God held him accountable to support his wife if he could, and it was even beginning to dawn on him that this included shielding her from his mother's cruel remarks. That would be the tough one, as he had let things go on for so long. He was spending time reading the Bible of late, and the passage he had just read came to mind. "Therefore a man shall leave his father and mother and be joined to his wife, and they shall become one flesh." Genesis 2:24 (NKJV). The words made their mark. "Leave...father...and...mother...join to his wife". The words stung, as he was painfully aware of how far he fell short of this. It was time to move on.

Making his way past the front hospital doors and staff, there was an emptiness settling within David. He already felt the loss of his daughter, and he was afraid to face his wife again. As he entered Kara's room, however, he quickly realized that his fear of rejection at Savannah's hand was unwarranted. Savannah ran into his arms, sobbing. Staff entered the room and removed the child, bed and all, wheeling her away, as the two clung to each other.

As he sat in the empty room, David's mourning reached its inward peak, and husband and wife cried together. Though neither acknowledged it, both were sure what the outcome would be. David visualized his little girl again, while a song of lament came over him. He heard himself singing the words softly in Savannah's ears.

Little whimpers in the night
Tiny fingers, hold them tight.
Quickly fading from our grasp,
Little ones, they grow so fast.

What is a child?
Who brings such joy?
The marvel of eternity,
A girl or a boy?

Silently molded
For greatness or pain,
Fleeting moments
Can't return again.

As autumn leaves,
The seconds fall
Till one may wonder
If they came at all.

These colored leaves,
None like the last,
Hold great secrets,
Future and past.

Lord guard my way
That when they go
These little ones
Your work will show.

Forgive the days when I forget
To cherish the gentle seed.
Honor instead the love we hold.
Meet every silent need.

May this work
You have begun
Never fail
But succeed

Savannah seemed to take some comfort in the words, though she did not understand why. They sat together, entwined for several hours, until the child was back in the room. Touching the face of this lifeless form, Savannah heard a song of her own. David cried as her soft voice formed the words.

If I could reverse
The toll of time
Again I'd hold
My baby's hand.   I'd hug her close
                            Upon my knee,
                         Treasure each smile,
                       Guard each breath
                     She drew with me.

I'd gather her tears
In a flask,
Let none escape my notice;
(Such a gentle task).
                        When tiny fingers
                        Stroked my brow,
                        I'd grasp the memory,
                        Value it now.

We would share secrets,
      She and I,
The pearls of wisdom
    That never die.

David quietly opened his Bible, looking for some source of
comfort for himself and his wife. There was just so much pain. But
they knew they had to let go. Kara was in Jesus' care now, and no
amount of crying or begging would change the news they were

about to receive. A small note was folded between those pages. It was a poem given to the couple on their wedding day. David always kept it in his Bible but had not read it since that day. As he opened it up, sensing this was the time for these words, David and Savannah read it together.

THE TWO BECOME
ONE

TODAY I WILL
COURT HER
TOMORROW
MY BRIDE,
MY LOVE,
MY COMPANION
ALWAYS
AT MY SIDE.

TODAY
MY SUITOR
TOMORROW
MY GROOM,
TO DWELL IN
MY HEART,
HIS CHOSEN
ROOM.

THOUGH BUTTERFLIES CEASE
OUR UNION
SHALL STAND,
A COVENANT ALWAYS
BY GOD'S COMMAND.

FORSAKING ALL OTHERS,
I NOW HOLD
HER FAST,
A UNION BEFORE GOD
REMAINING STEADFAST,
SHE IS
MY SISTER AND…

TAKING HIS HAND
I WILL NOT
LET HIM GO.
LAUGHTER OR TEARS,
I ASSURADLY KNOW
HE IS
MY BROTHER AND …

FOREVER MY FRIEND

May you find this union sacred,
Lasting a lifetime.

The couple held each other close, intertwined in their grief. Their tears mingled till one could not observe from whose face each tear flowed but only that there were plenty of them. Beyond the couple's notice, their Savior looked on as they comforted one another. His pleasure encompassed their unknowing soul. The union had been mended, as it ought always to have been. They had become one. They were free of the spirit of division that had raised its head against them. They had faced the darkness, and they won.

Chapter 6

Kara opened her eyes, gazing into the Face of her Lord. This time the words came from her lips. "Shall we go on? I want to be one with You, no matter what it costs. Just never stop holding me," pled the wounded child. He smiled, stroking her gently. Yes, they had to move on.

"Kara," He started. "Why were you so angry when you heard that the other children died?" He again knew just the right nerve to stroke.

Kara felt deeply ashamed. She knew that her anger was not a result of her concern for the others in the car. It was a covering for her own guilt for an accident that she was sure was her fault. "You know, Lord," she answered through the pieces of her shattered heart.

"They were a part of your eternal consequences, weren't they? They were a part of your bad choice, and you did not want to face that."

"Yes, Lord." The pain of the previous lesson was again deepening with an intensity that seemed to stuff her breath back into her chest. "That was why I was angry."

"The lesson required that it be painful, Kara, but the suffering was magnified by your own rejection of the truth. If you fall on My mercy, you will be broken. But if you reject the truth, you will be crushed." He paused, giving her time to drink this fully in and for the bitterness of it all to settle. "Instead you chose to blame it on Me."

Kara craved so deeply to undo what she had done, but she knew it was a craving that could never be satisfied. It would continue to burn in her forever. These last words now gashed into her even more severely, and she felt the lashes again. This time, however, she did not recoil. She knew they were just and that it was infinitely less than she deserved. There were lives lost, perhaps forever. And adding to the transgression, she had blamed the One Who had taken the sin of everyone upon Himself. If only she would have freely accepted His cleansing before, she would not be facing this now. She was not even sorry for herself anymore but rather that the sin had occurred at all, especially at her hands. "I am so sorry, Lord," she wept. "I am so sorry."

Jesus smiled, and the lashes subsided at least for the moment, but the memory was written in her heart as a testimony of what was done. "I know, child. I love you. We have much to do in your heart, but a time will come when this is all complete. Until then you must take your lashes, as all men must face their unrepentant sin, and I will take them with you, lest you be unable to bear them."

"How long?" she asked tearfully, pain searing into her being as a permanent friend. Somehow she knew these troubles were a trusted counselor which she must not despise, for in this was her healing.

"However long it takes," He answered. "The day will come when I wipe every tear from your eyes. But just know that this will continue however long it takes. I love you enough to do it right so that I will never lose you to the darkness again. It depends on you, child, but I am patient and in no hurry." He smiled a curious smile. "We have eternity, you know, and this is how you become one with Me." Then He pulled her close to His breast again. She was beginning to grasp His loathing of sin, as she welcomed their sufferings together as the only way to become one with her Friend.

"Lord," she began, now accepting the suffering before her, "if it is like this, and if suffering is good, shouldn't people just punish themselves on Earth before they get here?"

"Oh, no, child. That is both extensively damaging and fruitless. I took all the suffering for the sins of My people. Man's punishment is both cruel and ineffective, as he can only see through a dark clouded glass, covered with the smoke of sin and destruction. That is why it is so hideous to Me when I see how men torture each other and even themselves. To do so is an affront to Me. For a man to punish himself, he is communicating several sinful messages to Me. He is saying that he can judge himself more rightly than I, he is trying to avert My discipline that he has been commanded to love, and he is telling Me that My sacrifice was not enough for him. I ask only that he repent and allow Me to deal with the sin in his life, that he accept My sacrifice in His place. He must acknowledge both his sin and My saving grace to cleanse him. Child," He paused, as she braced herself, knowing by His kind hesitation that what would follow would be quite painful, "child, don't stiffen yourself against the suffering. You must embrace it, for it is your redemption." Kara started to weep again. "Child, the lashes are not for every sin you ever committed. If this were so, you would be engulfed in a raging fire that neither healed nor consumed you, a torment you truly could not bear. I took that punishment for you. You would be in the raging flames of Hell. The lashes are for the sins in which you relished even after you accepted Me as your Savior. They are for the sins of which you refused to repent. They are a result of rejecting My Sacrifice by continuing in them." Holding especially firmly to her hand, He continued. "As I told you, it is a loathsome thing in My sight when men punish and harm others. Kara, tell Me which sins pain you the most."

The lashes seemed to be coming in fury again. She knew she had not fully dealt with what she had to tell Him. "Well," she choked out between her gasps, "being angry at You and accusing You for my sins. And," she paused, the torment so intense, "remembering the night of the accident. Knowing that the other kids died and probably didn't know you. It was my fault. If I hadn't had to fight to get away from Daniel," she groped to form the words between the intense torment. "If I hadn't called him…", she could barely catch her breath as the lashes landed. She wanted desperately to stop, to blame someone else, but this was unthinkable. Even the inclination to do so intensified the thrashing. "They might not have lost control of the car!" she screamed. Her Master held her close, but the stripes continued, as she wailed in anguish. Chancing what she knew would not lighten the blows, Kara felt compelled to ask. "Was it all my fault? Wouldn't they have done it anyway?" As she anticipated, the pain intensified beyond belief, though this had not seemed possible. It was not a mere physical anguish, though that was a great part. Every part of her being seemed to cry out.

A sternness in His Voice, the Master replied, "The sins of the others make no difference in My dealings with you. If you choose to become a part of their sins, you are responsible for the whole of it. Their responsibility in the matter is of no consequence to you. I have made that clear in My Word. 'Lay hands suddenly on no man, neither be partaker of other men's sins: keep thyself pure.' 1 Timothy 5:22 (KJV) Kara," His Voice seemed to rumble, "is it your fault? Are you responsible for that night?"

"Yes, Lord!" she wailed. It seemed the pain would never end, and she understood that her words had been especially deplorable in His ears.

"Never again attempt to pass your stripes to another!" His Voice nearly roared. "It is given to you that I alone will take your lashes with you! You must never again seek to give them to another!" Her screams seemed to echo into an eternal vacuum. The fact that there was no time here exaggerated the impact of these happenings, as the suffering had an eternal quality that caused her to believe it would never end. Making matters worse, He seemed to lighten His hand from her and partake with her pain more at a distance. It was as if He were saying that as she had chosen to try to pass off her blame and suffering to others, she could no longer fully experience His comfort in it. The lashes had an illusion of being innumerable, yet each landed with such intensity that she was sure they had to be individually countable, as each left an eternal mark, each speaking a deafening message of the woes of sin.

"Lord!" she shrieked. "Please Lord, do not be so far from me! I am sorry! Please forgive me and come back to me!" Though He had withdrawn only a few feet, it seemed like an eternal chasm. Reaching out His hand, He pulled her to Himself. As she lay on His breast, the lashing continued, but in it she found a measure of peace. The tears intensified as she saw her lashes landing on her Lord's chest as well, but He only tightened His grip on her and held her to Himself.

"It is hard to remove the roots of sin," His Voice softened. "But there is no other way. It is meant to be dealt with in the body, before facing My eternal glory, over a life time. But men are shortsighted, and they refuse the healing. They do not welcome correction, which is their salvation. They refuse to rejoice when troubles come upon them to purge them. When they come to face Me, it all has to be done so intensely and completely, when they could have lessened the pain. Kara," He continued, "remember the lesson concerning the purity I have designed in relationships between a man and a women?"

"Yes, Lord." The intensity of the lashes subsided only a bit as she waited to hear Him speak.

"Remember the cutting of the mass of particles and the near impossibility of removing them?"

"Yes, Lord." The mention of those barbs jarred a memory that seemed to strengthen the force of the lashes again.

"Mankind joined with Satan in the garden of Eden, as surely as if it were a sexual union. The pieces of rebellion, hatred, and every type of sin entered into man. Particles of the most ghastly death and destruction were embedded into his being, and he became a vile creature, polluted by innumerable particles of evil. Every type of murder, rape, deception, and filth were deposited into him, buried between his very cells. His body had to die, lest he continue forever in that state. There was no redemption for him, Kara. Only through My sacrifice could his spirit and soul be saved. It was too late for his body. That would have to be made all over again, which is why at the resurrection, a new body is given."

"Then why are people responsible for that sin, if it is already in them?" she asked.

"It is a part of being a descendant of their father, Adam." He paused, seemingly to allow this to sink in. Kara desperately wished He would continue more quickly, as she felt the accusations rising up within her again. It seemed so unfair to inherit the sins of your parents. The lashes intensified once more, and though she knew she was wrong, she could not hide what was in her. The anger rising up was answered by the planting of blows, each more intense than her accusations, to cleanse them away. She knew He heard her unspoken indictments as fully as if she had shouted them.

"But indeed, O man, who are you to reply against God? Will the thing formed say to him who formed it, 'Why have you made me like this?' Romans 9:20 (NKJV) His Voice thundered. "Do you not inherit both what is helpful and what is evil from a parent?

Otherwise you could not exist at all! I have forgiven men, given them a way out. I willingly suffered for them. I died, taking their sin with all its horror and consequence, letting the sum of its fury rest upon Me, though I had committed no transgression. And even now, as you face the darkness you have chosen to keep from Me, I am taking the pain with you. Though you barely notice, each blow you receive is resting with much more strength upon Me. I have not passed the pain to others as you have. I have taken it all, and I have only allowed you to receive a miniscule portion, that you may never choose the darkness again. I have told you already that you would be destroyed if you received the blows for all your sins. Kara, what you are experiencing is but a tiny taste of My wrath against evil, as a segment of a single drop of water drawn from an endless number of immense oceans in comparison. You have tasted but a part of a drop from the cup of the wrath of God, Whose true size alone you cannot comprehend. Those who chose not to know Me must drink it all, Kara. Yet you continue to presume to argue against the goodness of God?"

The cries were coming from deep within her, from a depth of her being that seemed infinitely too far at her core to exist at all, let alone to have a voice. She could not fathom that this place in her even existed, such eternity that was enveloped in this tiny portion of her being. Or was this small place the entirety of her true personage? She could not tell. Stroke upon stroke, the beating seemed endless. She knew this sin held the blackness of all hatred and destruction, and she had been deeply marred by it. The desire to blame others

126

and pass the blows to them was so central to the sin nature of man! Though she thought she had repented as she apologized to her Maker, it had surfaced again.

"Adam blamed Eve in the garden," the Savior began to teach again. "He was willing to let her die for him rather than to own up to what he had done. Eve blamed the serpent for her choice to disobey Me. Parents have blamed their children, children their parents, husbands blame their wives, wives blame their husbands, and none is willing to fully face his own sin. This is hideous to Me, as is all sin that allows another to be its scapegoat, willing to pass its pain to another, is odious in My sight. From this comes all murder, torture, feuding, rapes, and every other vile thing. Once Adam had sinned, the Death was in him. All his attempts to pass it to another merely exaggerated the extent of the blackness of his soul. Only I can remove that, and it comes with the greatest of costs. I AM the only acceptable sacrifice. Yet men sit idly by, allowing sin to flourish like a well preserved garden, and take pleasure in the darkness. They nourish it like a pet. They court it like a lover. Is not their destiny well deserved if they refuse My redemption, the cross I bore for them? You continue to balk at the justice of Hell, where men choose to spend eternity without Me. Yet I have made a way of escape. I AM the Way of Escape, at the greatest of costs to Myself." His Voice resumed uncompromisingly. "Kara, I see your heart. I know it is still there. You may as well voice what is within you."

The blows were immense, but she had to speak it. He required her complete honesty. The words nearly tore through her throat. "It's still not fair! What about the people who have never heard about You?" It seemed as though her entire insides would burst out, and the torment did not subside. Lash upon lash, blow upon blow, the terror intensified.

Her Savior was still holding her close, and He seemed to keep her more tightly in His grasp than ever against His breast. She stole a glance from her position, buried in His arms. He was bleeding profusely from the lashes that she knew should have landed fully on her. No matter how painful this punishment that rested upon her, He received it infinitely more. She risked one look into His face to see rivers of tears falling from His pain stricken eyes.

"You are so small, so finite in your thinking," He began. "There is so much to answer that you cannot grasp. First, if I have commanded men to go, to spread My redemption to others, whose fault is it that some do not know? There are numerous men who profess My Name. If even a few followed Me completely and put their own sin aside, the work would be so great that there would be none who had not heard. Yet they continue to accuse Me of being unjust. They again indict Me, the Judge of the Universe, of judging unrighteously. Would it not be righteous if I held all the blood of the unreached to their account? Surely all men should be terrified to accuse Me, to even mention that so many have never heard My Name!" He again waited for these words to lodge deeply within her, cutting like large pieces of razors and planting what may be termed as the Fear of the Lord as they entered her very soul and spirit. "Secondly," He went on, "you show that you still do not trust My judgment against sin. All men are innately born with this darkness and have subsequently committed acts of evil deserving of death. Is My redemption owed to you? Am I the One who owes the debt that I am even required to save anyone? Who are these creatures who have the audacity to accuse God? And how do they dare to say I should let men come into My presence in any way they desire, when I paid so much to make a perfect way?" Kara waited, knowing there was more, preferring the lashes to the gashing words that were shredding her heart to bits. Yet she longed intensely to be one with her Lord, and she knew this was an integral part of the process. "Thirdly," His voice pierced into her consciousness, "do you actually believe that I do not find a way to give some type of opportunity to every man? Though I want to send My Church to rescue them, I AM the Savior of the world and have made a Way for every man. Just because you do not see it fully or understand, am I any less able to do this?"

Kara could only sob and allow the painful words to settle into her being. It overwhelmed her to know He was receiving every blow she received, and she impulsively started to push away from Him. "No!" his voice thundered, as He held her tightly. "I told you that you would not survive these blows alone! Never again shall you try to pull away from Me! You must take your lashes, knowing full well that they fall upon Me! This will not merely protect you, but it is also a constant reminder forever of the cost of sin! When we are finished, you will be marked forever that you never return to the hateful existence of its grasp! You will understand that there is no insignificant transgression against Me!" Kara lay in His grasp, sobbing and sobbing, every blow bringing a new lamentation for her evil heart. When the blows finally subsided, each had singly formed a unique indelible mark in her person that she knew could never be erased. How infinitely costly, she thought, was this luxury men so cherished called sin!

The Master gently laid her on a bed of rose petals, allowing her to rest for a time. But she yearned exceedingly for His touch and wanted nothing more than to be with Him. This was her Rescuer, this was her Love, and she would endure anything just to be with Him. Kara marveled at how far He had taken her, yet she was sure the sorrow was not nearly over yet. There was so much more to learn, and she was still acutely aware of the presence of sin.

"For there is nothing hidden which will not be revealed, nor has anything been kept secret but that it should come to light." Mark 4:22 (NKJV)

The Heart

Who can know,
Unless he rise up
And hear,
Lest he incline
His heart to understand?

Can the stone hill,
Silent before its maker,
Be witness to the
Greatness of God?

Can the power
Of the wind,
Roaring in fury,
Change its mind
When it has
No thought?

So man,
Determined to go
His own way,
Cannot cease to
Bring destruction
Upon himself.

He has set his face
Against God.

Yet the glory
Of the Son
Continues to
Offer the safety
Of His light,
Alternately a fire
Of comfort or fury
For those
In His presence.

Shall we
Stand against God?

Kara was enraptured in His presence as her Master lifted her out of the bed He had placed her in. She did not mind that there would be suffering. She only wanted Him. Tears of joy erupted at the sight of His approaching, in this place where there was no time. Everything was eternal, causing her period of waiting to feel excruciatingly long. She yearned for His lessons, anything to hear His Voice ripple through her being, and nothing else mattered.

"Kara." He had called her name! His Holiness swept over her, and she knew a lesson was starting again. "Kara, why do men pretend? They call evil good, and they justify sin in others as well as in themselves. They have become so wicked that they teach others there is no such thing as sin." There it was, her heart revealed again! "Kara, tell me about your friend Jackie." She had forgotten about this part of her life, how she had openly justified everything contrary to scripture. She wished that she could quickly forget it again.

"W…well," she stammered, already feeling the sting of the first lash, "she… uh… is…uh… g…gay."

"And you told her she was born that way. You told her that I made a mistake when I made her." He paused. "Is that true? Is it My fault she has gone this way?" He stopped a moment and proceeded, "And did it help her to tell her that? Did that help her to get free from her sin?"

The lashes were increasing, but Kara knew she had to answer, though the pain that would follow would surely take her breath away. "She felt that way since she was little," Kara protested. "Besides, a lot of her family is that way! What is so wrong with it anyway?" Kara was shocked by her own frankness in defending this sin, realizing that she could not hide what was in her. The explosion of blows was more than she expected, but they always were anyway. She felt as though the whips were reaching through her flesh to her very bone, but this again had to be. This was required to contend with her sin.

"Kara! Why do you incessantly continue to fight My precepts? Why must you continue to argue against My judgment? Do I not know all things?"

"Yes, Lord," she cried out, as the blows sunk deep into her inward parts, past the areas recognized by man. "I am sorry, but I still don't understand!"

"And because you do not understand, you can openly defy Me and help My creatures to remain in their fallen state? It is a very black crime to offer such an indulgence to people against Me, to help them die in their sin. You know what My Word says, yet you dare to argue against it. 'For this reason God gave them up to vile passions. For even their women exchanged the natural use for what is against nature.' Romans 1:26 (NKJV). This act is a complete mockery of the beauty I have created to propagate this earth. It is created by the evil one to laugh in My Face, and the unholy union that results from it causes damage you cannot see with your frail vision. The evil one would like to present a sexual union devoid of the possibility of life and reproduction. It is a sterile union, unable to create life or value. Men still believe they have a better way than Mine, though they are proved wrong over and over again. You helped her to be turned over to these vile passions when she could have cried out to be whole instead. You have again taken part in another's sin. 'But whoever causes one of these little ones who believe in Me to sin, it would be better for him if a millstone were hung around his neck, and he were drowned in the depth of the sea.' Matthew 18:6 (NKJV) It is no small thing in My sight when you cause one of My little ones to stumble! You are as guilty as if you performed the very acts yourself, and you are responsible for leading her further into the darkness!"

The torrent of blows increased, a fierce rage encased in each individual blow, and though Kara knew He was speaking the truth, a part of her resisted. Why could she not instantly give in to Him? The terror of the whips enveloped her as she waited for Him to speak again. Why did it seem to take so long? The agony would not relent. Yet He continued to let her wait as He remained silent and the lashes continued to land, over and over again. "Lord," she cried out, "how long till you speak to me again?"

"How long will Jackie suffer if she does not repent? What if she never gets saved? How long, Kara? Is your suffering anything compared to that?"

This seemed well beyond what she could take in. These whips carried a fury fed by what seemed a very torrent of wrath. All she could do was scream, as the venom of what she had done soared endlessly throughout her form. "I am sorry, Lord!" she wailed.

"Sorry? Sorry that it still hurts you, or sorry for the damage you have done? Kara, the treachery of sin is embodied in selfishness. Do you have a right to have sex with a boy because that desire is in your sin nature? Can you steal without consequence because you were taught by a parent how to do it? The sin nature is expressed in many ways, and none is insignificant. Just because the desire is present does not make you free to follow it. What if you desire to kill someone? Would that mean it was My fault if you carried out the evil act, that it was because I had made you that way? You helped Jackie take her identity in her sin, to believe that this sin actually defines who she is, which will make it much harder for her to break away from. I love Jackie, and I did not make her sin." As though letting this sink in, He was silent. Lash after lash ripped at her being. Though He was holding her, she barely felt His presence, the pain was so intense. "You again blame Me for the sin of My creation. Should I have taken away free will and possessed robots instead of friends?"

The words landed as barbs within her, each carrying a fire that could not be extinguished. "I really am sorry, Lord," she continued. Nearly afraid to allow the words to escape her but unable to stop them, she asked, "Will she ever come back and ask you to come into her heart?" She could feel His arms holding her again, and she wept exceedingly as she saw his bloody arms, cut and marred, as He had been holding her all the time.

"That is something not given for you to know," He answered, as she continued to writhe in this incessant pain. "Instead you must take this lesson with all its hideous detail that you never forget the gravity in My sight when you willfully cause another to stumble into sin." He was silent at that point for some time, holding her firmly against His chest, as the lashes landed, over and over again. It seemed impossible, yet each left a new mark in her soul, writing His words in indelible ink, deep red ink. They were written in His blood. When the thrashing subsided, she could still feel their venom, yet in His forgiveness, she felt a sweet release.

"Lord?" she started, weeping. "Am I such an evil child that this had to happen? Am I worse than most people? Or does this happen to everyone?"

"Kara, all have this disease called sin. But you must never compare yourself with anyone. All are totally wretched in their sin, flawed beyond measure; but how I deal with others is of no consequence to you. This is how you must face your sin. This is your deliverance. You have been given much, and thus you carry a greater responsibility for your refusal to accept My correction. When you willingly sin, with full knowledge of what you are doing, you cause this darkness to be more completely embedded into your soul. The longer you refuse Me, the deeper the blackness forms and takes hold within you. Thus removing these things which you would not allow My blood to cleanse on Earth becomes a horrible task When men run quickly to My mercy for their sins, much of this is not necessary. They have already learned to face their sins, and when they stand before Me, much of what remains to remove can simply drop off in My presence, if they are willing. Though there may still be intense work involved, as I scourge every son I receive (Hebrews 12:6), it need not be this cruel suffering, for they have learned to agree with Me quickly and to fully repent. Many have accepted much of that scourging through the things they willingly suffer on Earth. But when you bring sin into My very presence, there is a high cost. It becomes a blatant affront to Me, and I cannot deal with it in the kindness I would like to for your sake. The only reason you do not understand this is that you have refused to consider how utterly despicable sin actually is. Men believe that they can somehow escape the consequences of their actions, and they spend endless hours conniving, trying to hide their transgression. They think if no one on Earth sees their darkness, I will wink at it Myself and not hold it to their charge. They do not understand that it is My mercy that allows them to get caught on Earth and My compassion that causes them to receive retribution at the hands of governments and of other men. For if the consequences of his feeble existence bring a man to repentance, what a precious gift he has received! For no matter how much men argue their case, sin will not be allowed to dwell with Me. There are absolutely no exceptions."

"Does that mean that when people have problems or sicknesses that You don't heal right away, it's because of something bad they have done? Is it their fault? What about Job?" she asked.

"No, child, that is not it at all. But all these troubles are a result of the sin problem in one form or another. I use these delays to purify My people from the sin nature that exists in them from birth, in My wisdom knowing that it is much better to deal with these things before they leave the body. But I also heal in order to teach as well. There are many reasons why this occurs, but what My children often miss in their understanding is that I am much more interested in the eternal results of a thing than in their temporal comforts. I love them, and sometimes in that love, My decisions are not what they want them to be at the time. Do not even earthly parents delay the gratification of their children's desires in order to protect them from their own impulsiveness? How much more shall their perfect Father decide what is best to accomplish His purposes in them? Yet if they will allow themselves to be trained by these things, if they will rejoice in their sufferings, the benefit is without measure. They too often fight My very purposes, refusing to accept that I know what is best."

"So is it wrong to ask for healing or for bad circumstances to change?" she continued. "If it is just a delay, why do people still die from their sicknesses? Also, lots of people say when you don't get what you ask for, it is because you don't have any faith at all."

"Of course it is not wrong to ask. It is actually commanded. It is a part of dependence on Me. But it must be accompanied by trust, even as I trusted My Father. This is relayed to you in My Word, speaking of My prayer before I was crucified. I did not enjoy the pain and suffering either, but I left that decision to My Father Who I trusted to administer exactly what was necessary. Even now, as you receive your lashes, you must trust Me in the same way, knowing that what is administered is for your welfare, lest you be unable to abide in My presence. 'He went a little farther and fell on His face, and prayed, saying, "O My Father, if it is possible, let this cup pass from Me; nevertheless, not as I will, but as You will. "' Matthew 26:39 (NKJV) Have I not clearly stated that each man has a cross to bear, that he must take up his cross and follow Me? 'Then He said to them all, "If anyone desires to come after Me, let him deny himself, and take up his cross daily, and follow Me.' Luke 9:23 (NKJV) But men have been unwilling to follow in My footsteps, preferring an easier way. There is no easy way. 'Enter by the narrow gate; for wide is the gate and broad is the way that leads to destruction, and there are many who go in by it.' Matthew 7:13 (NKJV) And if someone dies and joins Me, he is healed, as he receives a new body. As for faith, I have never asked My children to have faith in the things I give. That is misplaced faith. Their faith is to be in Me, trusting My love above their circumstances." His very words seemed as fire that caused the rebellion still in her to burn with a searing flame, ripping through her soul as a mighty, ruthless storm. Yet in her love for Him, she felt satisfied. The discourse had captured her breath and gripped at her very soul as she listened on. Her heart began to sing a silent song, His Voice alternately answering her.

Capture my heart, Lord,
I'm empty inside
Capture my heart
Don't want to hide.

Darkness engulfs me,
please bring me out,
I don't even know
What this is all about.

I know your agony,
Understand your pain
Hold on to My hand
Be free of the stain.

Capture my heart, Lord,

Make my soul fly!
Capture my heart
Don't know how to try.

Receive My refreshing,
I've not let you go
You are still mine
I want you to know.

Can't help my feelings
forgot how to cry
Capture me Lord
I don't want to die.

Capture my heart
can't seem to hold on
Rescue me quickly
Before faith is gone.

One day you'll behold Me
My glory you'll see
Then you'll understand
What I made you to be.

Don't know how this started
Just want it to end
Capture my heart
I'm willing to bend.

Let Me capture you now,
Your heart, soul, and mind
That this day would end
With the darkness behind.

Let healing flow o're you
Your time has come
For comfort, refreshing,
Your day in the Son.

Capture my heart, Lord.
I choose to believe
It's You Who have comfort
My soul to relieve.

"Kara," He commenced, "what are you thinking now?"

"Well," she started, knowing He was the only one Who possessed any true answers, "I am thinking of the little first grade girl in my school that hung herself last year. Lord, what about people who commit suicide? Do they automatically go to Hell? What if it is a little kid like Peggy?"

"All final judgment is in My hands, Kara, and only I know a person's heart. My decision is based on what is in the heart of a man rather than on a simple set of rules. It is true that this act is hideous to Me, as is any destruction of the life I have created. But only I know the full accountability of every creature, what he understands, and his ability to control his own actions. These acts stem from wickedness indeed and are inspired by the very powers of darkness. Each person will stand before Me and face what he has chosen to do with the life that I created. It is no small thing when he squanders what I have provided, and he will certainly face his sin. But for you it is not given to judge the fate of such a one. For you it is given simply to trust that I am just and merciful. For surely you understand by now that I love My creation. Kara, from what you know of My character, where do you think Peggy is?"

"I think she is with You, Lord," she replied softly.

"What else, Kara? What else were you thinking about?" He prodded.

"Well," she started, anticipating the stinging words before they began, "why don't You stop bad things? You are so big, yet You let such bad things happen. What about terrorist attacks that kill so many people? Why don't you stop them?"

"Are you thinking of September 11, 2001, Kara? Are you accusing Me of injustice again?" He asked. Though her heart stung with the correction and she felt the scourging of each word He spoke, she had to hear His answer, so she pushed on.

"So many people were killed," she pleaded, knowing He saw her heart. "Why did it have to happen?" It was again as if someone were taking a giant scouring instrument and scrubbing her insides until they were raw and bleeding, cleansing away her accusations against Him.

"This particular evil did not have to happen, though many things must occur before the end has come. It was the result of the hearts of evil men. Yet it is clear that much evil will take place in this world, in order that both good and evil may be fully manifest and the truth be made known. '…It is impossible that no offenses should come, but woe to him through whom they do come!' Luke 17:1b (NKJV) I heard the screams of every man and every woman. I felt the anguish of every family member left behind. Many that did escape this disaster were led by My Spirit and were caused to miss perishing in the event, though some did not even recognize that it was My doing at all. Men have insisted for years that I not be a part of the nation in which you live. They have rejected Me on every side, ridiculing solid teaching. 'For the time will come when they will not endure sound doctrine, but according to their own desires, because they have itching ears, they will heap up for themselves teachers; and they will turn their ears away from the truth, and be turned aside to fables.' 2 Timothy 4:3-4 (NKJV) Why are they so surprised that evil comes upon them? They have pushed Me away and refused My help, yet they have the audacity to sit in judgment of Me when I do not act on their behalf in the way that they desire. Those who truly love Me accept the suffering as a gift from My Hand, and in so doing, they receive great reward. Yet even in the midst of this tragedy, I reached out My hands of comfort and salvation to all that would come, to those who would call on My Name. As I have told you before, I have given free will to mankind. I do not want man to select darkness, but some have chosen to use their lives on Earth to propagate evil in spite of My wishes. This occurs that it may be made known who each person has chosen for his eternal companion. Notice My words concerning some of them. 'You are of your father the devil, and the desires of your father you want to do. He was a murderer from the beginning, and does not stand in the truth, because there is no truth in him. When he speaks a lie, he speaks from his own resources, for he is a liar and the father of it.' John 8:44 (NKJV) My Word also explains that even My people suffer injustice in this life, that all things might be fulfilled. 'They will put you out of the synagogues; yes, the time is coming that whoever kills you will think that he offers God service.' John 16:2 (NKJV) Yet others hear My call and obey My Voice, some even sacrificing their own lives that others might survive during these horrific happenings. This has proved for many to be a refining fire that has caused them to shine before Me as pure gold, and they shall not lose their reward. Those that cried to Me during this time were met by My love and redemption, if they chose to receive it. Is it not merciful if this time of horror leads a man to repentance? As I have said before, I am much more interested in the eternal results of a thing than for that which is temporal, though the agony of My creation is of great consequence to Me." The lashes stung, but in His comfort, Kara finally accepted His kindness in His dealings with man, and the correction seemed much lighter upon her for a time. A poem came to her mind.

The buildings crashed,
The people fell.
A city looked
Very much like Hell...

The fires raged
And anger grew,
Yet under the rubble
Is something new...

Not merely chaos
But a well thought out plan.
Out of evil comes good
From our God unto man.

Go forward, march on,
Through the restlessness of life;
Let evil not be our ruler
Nor our end be in strife.

For God is the Maker
Of one and of all;
Though rulers may rise,
They one day will fall...

Let us fall on our faces
Before God, Who has grace,
Before Jesus, the Savior
Of this human race.

A story to be told,

A lesson to be learned;

Divine intervention

Completely unearned.

A tale for the young,

News to the old.

It cannot be forgotten

But must continue to be told.

"What else, Kara? You were not finished. You still desire to accuse Me," He stated. The scouring continued in her soul as she proceeded in this vein, scrubbing away at the blame in her heart. Though she felt totally raw, she knew there was no way of avoiding this confrontation. She had compiled so many charges against Him, and they must be answered.

"If you love people so much, why are so many people killed in the Old Testament? Why were the Israelites commanded to kill even the women and the babies? Why was everything so much harsher in that time? It makes a lot of people doubt You and think that You are mean." The lashes were landing again, as He knew her heart.

"You mean it makes YOU doubt Me," He answered. "It is YOU who are condemning My actions as cruel and unnecessary. It makes YOU think that I am mean. Why must you continually pass off your darkness to others?" The lashes were coming in a fury again, not because she had asked a question, but rather because she had chosen again to assign her blame to others. This sin had buried itself so very deeply within her that it had become an integral part of her, and it again raised its ugly head in defiance of the Master. She was both accusing Him and attempting to voice her indictments through the mouths of others, hiding behind their unknown faces. He remained silent for a time, allowing the stripes to reach into her soul to answer her defiance. Though she cried out, He waited to answer, that this darkness would truly be blotted out from among her members. The scourging must persist until this was ripped from her.

After a time, He began speaking again, though the lashes continued to land. "We are getting deeper, Kara, into your very being. This blackness must be removed. Though your questions present an air of innocence, We both know what is in your heart. As for My severity shown in the Old Testament, you have already been shown My loathing of sin. The Old Testament is a fantastic picture of the penalties, as this occurred before My Sacrifice was complete in man's stead. The women and the children of these populations were already polluted beyond measure, and the sin of their heritage was buried deeply within them. If they were allowed to propagate, they would have produced increasingly sinful creatures, as became apparent when Israel disobeyed Me in these commands, allowing those that were to be destroyed to live. Those that they refused to deal with became a thorn in their side, even as your unrepentant sins have become a distress unto you. Sin must be dealt with in a ruthless manner, showing no compassion on its evil designs. Those that can be saved I spare, but only I see the heart of a man. If you notice, the instructions were explicit, differing from one population to the next according to My wisdom concerning the specific evil needing to be destroyed. Why must men continue to mock Me in this, as though they understand better than I what is good and what is just? Is it not more merciful that I remove these beings from the earth before more are born among them to enter the furnace of Hell? All have sinned and deserve death. There are no exceptions among men. Is it not better that I diminish the damage? Again you pass judgment, not understanding My dealings with man. The fate of those who fell is in My hands. Should I have waited until they were beyond repair? There is consequence for sin, and that fact remains a constant in the laws of the universe. I AM holy, and that does not change." The words landed like barbs into her flesh, barbs that cut and pulled at her very being, as she listened on.

"We must get past this, Kara, for 'The fear of the LORD is the beginning of wisdom; …' Psalms 111:10a (NKJV). An understanding of the blackness of sin is the starting point. I used the events in the Old Testament to show this. Even as you are receiving your lashes, the earth during this time was getting correction for sin. I was tearing away the darkness, preparing the ground for My merciful coming. Even then men could come to Me, trusting in the Sacrifice for which the world had to wait, as I tilled the soil that all would not be lost. This had to be done, in order that I might come and redeem them, that they would recognize their need for a Savior. For as it has been written, 'Therefore the law was our tutor to bring us to Christ, that we might be justified by faith.' Galatians 3:24 (NKJV) Kara, you must take this to heart, understanding My utter distaste for sin. None deserves to be redeemed at all. I do not owe this to any man. I redeem them because I love them, and My mercy is abundant to all who would come, but I will absolutely not tolerate sin. It destroys everything in its path." Kara cried as the words penetrated her heart. She knew He was just. Why was it so difficult to accept His complete abhorrence of sin? Was it not because she still clung to its evil desires in many ways? The lashes subsided as she rested in His arms, those magnificent arms that took so much of her suffering, the precious limbs that received the pain of what she had done.

"Why does it seem like the New Testament is so much gentler," she asked. "I know you still hate sin. What makes things so different now?"

"Do you still not understand that what I do among men is always geared to their redemption? Though they do not recognize it, all I do is because of My love for mankind. My coming to earth, My Sacrifice in the place of men changes everything. The cross is a point of pivot for the men of this earth, a turning point signifying absolute repentance. Just as I deal with you now, I allow only what is needed to change your heart, because you are already forgiven in Me. I have not changed at all, as I AM God. It is the plight and position of man that has changed through My Sacrifice and the redemption I have given. Why does man continue to complain that he receives the benefit from what has already been done in the earth?

Do I not have the right to do with My creation what I deem best? Those who benefit complain because it exposes their love affair with sin. It is not that they have compassion on others as they pretend. This realization exposes their very sinfulness, and men desire to hide from it. They choose to continue in the darkness rather than to embrace My correction that is designed to bring them deliverance. Though I walked with sinners and prostitutes on this earth, I still commanded repentance, as they were instructed to '…go, and sin no more.' John 8:11b (KJV) I showed them My uncompromising love, yet making it abundantly clear that I did not condone their sin. When people met Me, they were convicted, as Zacchaeus was. Is it an unrepentant man who answers as he did, 'Look, Lord, I give half of my goods to the poor; and if I have taken anything from anyone by false accusation, I restore fourfold.'? Luke 19:8b (NKJV) Kara," He continued, "are you willing yet to stop hiding behind others, to cease passing off your sins? You know that I see into your very being." Nodding her head, she wept from deep within her soul, the scouring within her scrubbing all her objections away.

"Kara," He began again. "I want you to sit with Me." Climbing fully into His lap, she tearfully looked into those magnificent eyes that shone clearer than anything she had ever seen. "Kara," He proceeded, "what do you think your purpose is?" She paused, not sure how to answer.

"Well, uh, … to get people saved I suppose? And maybe my art?"

"Those are functions, Kara. Men confuse function with purpose. From the beginning of time, man's purpose has been to be in relationship with the Father. When Satan destroyed that in the garden, the result was man without purpose. In his ignorance, man is constantly trying to discover his purpose. Without a relationship with God, he attempts this by defining himself by his function." His Voice ceased momentarily in order to allow her to absorb these thoughts. "Kara, this may seem harmless enough, but actually the results are disastrous. Though men are allowed to serve many functions, like the ones you just mentioned, your true purpose never changes. Function is temporary, but purpose is eternal. When a man believes, however, that his function is his purpose, he can become desperate and capable of untold evils when these functions change or appear to be lost. He may sink into severe despondency or even resort to a survival mode to try to regain what he feels his purpose is. If, for example, a spouse leaves and one's purpose is defined in that relationship, a human is capable of rage and murder. If he thinks his purpose is in his vocation, he may go to any lengths to keep that position, resorting to all kinds of sin. You have heard stories of hospital workers who intentionally harmed others in order to get the satisfaction of rescuing them afterwards, even giving babies lethal drugs that they might be able to resuscitate the child afterwards. This is an example of what can occur when purpose and function become confused. If the worker has no emergency, which he believes is his purpose, he creates the disaster himself. As you can see, the consequences of this thinking are completely unacceptable."

Allowing this to settle into her spirit, the Master resumed His teaching. "Wanting others to get saved is noble enough, though only I can draw them. You can bring My Word and My love, but I must do the rest. But even this is not your purpose. Or what will happen when all that will be saved have come? Would you re-introduce sin to maintain your purpose? Thus you will be without purpose again. Kara, your purpose is to be in relationship with Me." Kara lay her head on His chest, loving just to hear His Voice.

"But what about your art, Kara?" The words began to sting. "What if you could never paint again? What if you had no strength in your arms? Would you still love Me? And would you be angry?" She sensed the whips as they rustled in readiness, awaiting a single command to begin again. They had assembled especially for this moment, proclaiming by their very presence a gravity beyond all things she had faced up to this time. "I don't know," she started, feeling the rod of correction coming to attention. "Yes, I would be very angry!" The words barely left her lips as He nodded for the thrashing to begin again. "You can't take my art!" she screamed. "It's all I have to express myself!" At this the whips landed in full rage, as she gasped for her breath, still not willing to give in. She was angry even at the question, that he would require of her this most precious thing.

"Kara." His voice was gentle but unyielding. "You have placed another god before Me. This is indeed a great sin." She wailed as the flogging went on, yet she would not relent. This went far deeper than anything up to this point. She had claimed this prize, and her rage seethed, as the stripes deepened to a point that she felt would surely destroy her. He sat silently, waiting for the flogging to bring her to repentance, as she cried out in anguish. This would be a very long process. He had touched the very nerve of every piece of defiance that remained in her, and it was refusing in an unearthly fury to let go. Until she joined Him in the battle, the lashing of the whips must go on. These marks must truly hit the very depths of her being to extinguish this evil from her forever.

"Kara," He continued, "it is not enough even if you chose to make Me more important than your art, and you have refused to do even that. You must give it up completely." This seemed an incredible affront, a demand beyond reason. She had scarcely considered the former, but the later was entirely too much. She cried and wailed as the beating tore through her frame, but she would not relent. He continued without interruption. "Men have heard that it is necessary to place nothing before God in importance in their lives. They learn that doing so is equivalent to the idolatry for which Israel was so often reproved. Thus a man is encouraged to check his priorities. Kara, it is not about a list of priorities. There is no list in relationship with Me. In relationship with Me, nothing else is of any importance. I must be able to take everything away at any time, without notice, and your love for Me must remain untouched by resentment. When I say to you to put no god before Me, it doesn't merely mean to keep it at a lower level. The instruction means that none of your gods should appear before My face, in front of My vision. You know I see everything, so it means you can have no other gods at all. Men clutch tightly to their vices and sins, believing that as long as they keep them at a lower level than Me on their imaginary list of priorities, they are justified in nurturing them. They become deceived into believing that they can somehow control these things, but they are still before My face. They are flaunting their gods, parading them before Me, and it is deplorable in My sight. Thus the war on sin is never complete."

The flogging persisted, as she writhed beneath the blows. Her rage was diminishing only a little bit, as each lash seemed to tear another piece of it from her, shredding and ripping her very soul, but she still did not want to let go. She scarcely felt His arms about her, barely knew He was even there, though if she had looked, he held her firmly still. On and on, the whips landed, yet she did not give in. On and on the scourging continued, and she continued to resist. With fury the rod met her, her defiance mocking Him still. This was the gravest of all correction, as she did not relent. His Voice began again, this time with an anguish of eternal terror. "So this is your choice?" He cried. "Your art rather than Me? Shall I stop and leave you in your sin?" His words held the power of an eternal haunting. "I will not abide other gods any more than a husband will allow his wife other lovers! You can not have both!" She could feel His tears falling into her wounds, stinging as a thousand flaming swords.

Kara screamed in terror, realizing at this moment the gravity of what He had spoken. "NO!" she screamed. "NO! Don't ever go away!"

"So what is your choice, Kara? I will not abide in the presence of another god!"

Kara wailed, mourning the loss before the words escaped her mouth. "I want YOU, Lord! You can take my art!" Hesitating just a bit, she continued. "But why do I have to give it away? What's wrong with my art?" The flogging went on as she waited for Him to explain.

"The art is no longer yours, Kara. It was a talent granted by Me for your use, a work you have done. When I gave it to you, it was pure and good. But you polluted it when you made it your god, as now is fully manifest. It is as much a god to you as the golden calf was to the children of Israel in the desert, as much and more! You have sought your art when you would not seek Me. And now you have placed it so high that you were nearly willing to give Me up to keep it. It is hideous to Me! Because you clutched to this so tightly, I never want to see it in your hand again! This will not be restored to you!" The weeping deepened into utter dismay as the child now accepted the stripes without a fight. She lay in a chasm of endless darkness, taking her lashes without complaint. She knew this had been the most grievous battle of all. She saw visions of the things she had painted, shredded and burned in her sight. Piece upon piece appeared before her, even those in her imagination that she had not painted yet. Each was consumed in her own fury, the defiance to which she had clung. Her paints in all their colors were consumed in a vehemence of judgment. It was her greatest loss, yet she knew it was a loss to be desired above all the lessons. She truly welcomed the thrashing of the whips, as what they were etching into her person with each fierce stroke was of more value than her very life and being. Those eternal words proclaimed that she was fully His and He was hers. The work continued endlessly through a long eternal night. She knew she could not be spared any of this agony. This darkness had to be fully dealt with, leaving no trace behind. When the flogging subsided, Kara fell fast asleep entwined in Her Saviors arms. He whispered softly to her spirit as she slept, the agony in His Voice still apparent. "This was the most costly of all battles, Kara. It was a war for your very soul. You must never, never forget." He stroked her face and gently took an eternal pen, filled with His blood, and carved forever His Name across her forehead. She was truly His, and the powers of darkness would know her no longer.

"Now if anyone builds on this foundation with gold, silver, precious stones, wood, hay, straw, each one's work will become clear; for the Day will declare it, because it will be revealed by fire; and the fire will test each one's work, of what sort it is. If anyone's work which he has built on *it* endures, he will receive a reward. If anyone's work is burned, he will suffer loss; but he himself will be saved, yet so as through fire." 1 Corinthians 3:12-15 (NKJV)

Chapter 7

Kara awakened to a brightness about her. She looked up at the Savior holding her in His arms. She drew in a deep breath in awe as for the first time she looked fully into His face. The air stung her passageways, as the lashes had left their marks within and without, but there were no new stripes. She felt the marks within her, reminding her that she was still alive, still alive in Him, and she cherished their work. She had only seen His face in part before, and the sight held her in its wonderful grasp.

"Kara," she heard Him call to her. Kara did not care what transpired now, as long as she could be with Him. If she received every lash again a thousand times over, it would be of no consequence. She would welcome anything at His hand as a cherished gift. Kara truly trusted that anything He did was an expression of His love for her, and she was content. "Kara," He repeated, "it's time to take a bath." She giggled at the words, not comprehending what He could possibly mean. Her heart was much lighter, and she was a girl in love. Looking down at her form, she was a bit saddened as she saw her flesh torn and marred beyond human recognition. How could she still be beautiful to Him?

"Ok, Lord." She wondered what this ritual would bring.

"I am washing you first in My Blood," He continued, not even acknowledging her laughter. "Kara, it will be like a baptism. I must place you completely under the blood." She understood what He was referring to now, as she had always been afraid to have her face submerged before. But she trusted Him and was willing to accept this at His hand. A giant tub was placed before them, filled with His Blood, for the cleansing of the nations. She began to hear the voices of many angels worshipping their Lord as the blood covered her entirely, except for her face. As He placed her face under as well, submerging her completely, a panic tried to ensue, but she pushed it away. He held her under long, as His blood was filling every crevice; but when she would have breathed, He did not let her up. She had to trust Him. "Kara," she heard Him say, "breathe in the blood. Allow it to fill you completely." Kara opened her mouth and lungs, not knowing if she would drown, and let it flow in. She felt the blood infuse her very being with life, and she could breath freely of it. Lifting her out, He told her, "Kara, we are not done yet."

Another tub was presented before them. "I am washing you in the water of My Word," He continued. "Kara, this is another baptism. I must place you completely under the water." Again she trusted Him and was willing to receive anything from Him. This tub was filled with water that looked like liquid crystal, with precious gems scattered throughout. There were diamonds and rubies, topaz and sapphire, emeralds and jasper, and stones without number, many of which she did not recognize. Sweet perfumes and spices were blended in the water as He gently lifted her in. The water offered searing pain, as it flowed into her wounds, cleansing all in its way. As He submerged her completely, He held her under long, and His word was filling her being; she again had to breathe it into her lungs, swallowing it into her belly, and He did not let her up. She had to trust Him. "Allow it to fill you completely." She felt the water infuse her very being with life, and she could breath again without restraint. It no longer hurt to breath, as He was healing every part of her. Though its cleansing brought pain, she did not mind. She knew His word was being written in her, etched into every crevice of her eternal being. As He lifted her out of the water, Kara looked at her limbs. Her skin was more pure than a new born baby's skin, with only faint marks where the lashes had been. "Kara," He said softly, "I will not take them all away yet. These marks must remain for a time as a reminder of what has been." Though the words stung deeply, leaving an eternal sadness, the rapture of being in His presence was far greater.

"Kara," He continued. "We have one more baptism. This is the baptism of fire. This is My Holy Spirit." Kara trusted her Lord, ready to accept any suffering He placed upon her, and followed Him willingly to that place. There was a huge and mighty fire, and she knew this was the ultimate test of her trust and love for Him. Even if these were the very fames of Hell, she must obey. Taking her hand, He lead her. To all who looked on, she was beautiful beyond belief, enough to take away the breath of a thousand men. As they walked into the flames, she felt no fear. He was holding her hand. The fire removed all doubt as it filled her lungs and reached into her heart with a power and authority she did not yet understand. She was enthralled in His love, and she drank of it without reservation. It seemed they had been in the fire a long while, embracing, laughing, and crying together. This was a dance in His presence, and though the fire burned within her, it was not a flame of torment at all. It was instead as a river of passion, a love for the nations and for all people. As the two walked from that spot, the fire followed, and it clothed them. The Savior placed a white robe upon her, and the marks were visible only to her and to her King. Yet they both knew what those marks meant and the eternal cost that was paid to wear them. They were now treasures, with a sweet aroma oozing from each of them, each a costly jewel any with understanding would relish to wear. One lash had landed on her ring finger, the only one visible to all. As she looked upon it, it became the most beautiful pale green jewel she had ever seen. "This is your engagement ring," He whispered. "The wedding is yet to come."

....

David and Savannah sat nervously in Kara's room, waiting for the doctor to come and explain the results of the brain studies. Their hands were clutched together tightly, as they anticipating either a speck of hope or the slap of defeat. "David," Savannah's raspy voice started, "I don't think I can do this!", and she tightened her grip. Pulling her head to his chest, the man comforted his wife the only way he knew how. She cried in his arms, glad at least that he had chosen to join her in this sorrow. Their daughter lay motionless, the sounds of the breathing machine filling the silence.

A tall, slender brown-haired young man entered the room, appearing no more than thirty years old. "Mr. and Mrs. Tells?" he began. The couple looked up, searching the eyes of this man who seemed to hold the fate of all they held dear. "We have the studies back." His hesitation brought a fierce dread neither of the couple had ever known. "We found little or no discernable brain activity." He allowed the gravity to completely engulf them. "I have to recommend that the machines be turned off." Though David had believed he was prepared for this, it dropped as a giant boulder within him, and Savannah's heart sunk to a despair beyond imagination. "The insurance will allow this kind of care for five more days, to give you preparation time. But after that, unless you have some other source of payment, the rescue efforts have to stop." David just looked at the man, unable to speak. "Shall we continue for the five days?" he went on relentlessly. David nodded, and the man exited the room.

Husband and wife held each other tightly, unable even to cry. The silence was heavy upon them, but there was no strength to speak. Both had secretly hoped against hope that this would not be the answer, that God would return their child. The thought of funeral arrangements were beyond them. It would all have to wait. Savannah was the first to succeed in forcing away this weighty stillness, as she fell fully into David's arms and cried. They wept together for hours, hospital staff occasionally looking on. Some were moved with compassion as others just shook their heads, feeling that the mourning should have been complete by now. After all, it had been nearly nine months. Surely they knew how all this would end. Savannah continued her endless vigil at Kara's bedside, as she released her husband from her grasp so that he could go home and rest.

Savannah barely heard the door open, as she looked up to see the handsome young man enter the threshold of the room. There stood Jeremy, cautiously approaching, and her tears could not be hidden from him. Savannah felt an extra stab of torment at the knowledge that she had spent very little time with him of late. Here he stood, her trusting, loving son who had so desperately needed a mother. She felt she had failed him once again. Oblivious to her thoughts, he pulled her into his arms. "I know, Mom. They told me," he whispered. Savannah was struck by his kindness, wondering at this young man who had been given so little at her hand, that he had never withheld his love from her, that he bestowed the full honor of being a mother on her without reservation. Who was this young man? He joined in her silent vigil, never once requiring her to speak. Such a precious gift, this boy that the enemy had sought to destroy before he was born! Intermittently, he would hold her again, whenever she started to cry, frequently with tears flowing down his own cheeks as well. "I am sorry I never got to know her," he whispered. "She looks like an angel lying there."

As Savannah looked upon the child, her eyes were opened. She saw what Jeremy saw. Kara's face was fairly glowing behind all the machines. Her words escaped nearly as a gasp. "She is with Jesus!" she exclaimed. Walking over to Kara, she kissed her face. Then turning to Jeremy, she donned a faint smile, as she was free to love again. Savannah spoke with her son, asking him about all the little things that were happening in his life. He told her about his struggles in losing his job, the neighbor he witnessed to that morning, and of the things that concerned him. It was mostly small talk, but at least it was talk, as it brought healing to a young man.

....

"Kara, why do men spend so much time hiding their flaws from others?" asked the Savior, His eyes turned towards the princess sitting beside Him in her long, flowing white robe. "Why do they work so hard, and develop so much skill, simply to evade the truth?"

"You know, Lord," she uttered softly, her head against His chest. She remained still, absorbing the majesty of His form, the gentleness of His touch, and the rippling of His Voice, simultaneously memorizing the scent of His love.

"Yes, Love," He continued. "But I want to hear you say it."

The smile on her face turned to a beaming radiance, as she began to glow. "Well, I used to think that privacy was a right, that no one was entitled to know what was in me, especially if I felt that what was there was bad. I was afraid that if I told certain things, people would not love me. Some things seem so very dark before you say them, even though when you finally do, they become quite small in the light. But most of all, I think men hide their sins because they do not want to let them go."

He smiled at her, pleased with the insight with which she spoke. "You have learned your lessons well. Men do not recognize the battle in which they live, that their very souls are at stake. I am a God of light, and in Me is no darkness. Men who come to the Light desire to be free from their sins, but when they hide in the darkness, their actions are professing their allegiance to the system of evil. I instructed them in 1 John 1:5-9, 'This then is the message which we have heard of him, and declare unto you, that God is light, and in him is no darkness at all. If we say that we have fellowship with him, and walk in darkness, we lie, and do not the truth: But if we walk in the light, as he is in the light, we have fellowship one with another, and the blood of Jesus Christ his Son cleanseth us from all sin. If we say that we have no sin, we deceive ourselves, and the truth is not in us. If we confess our sins, he is faithful and just to forgive us [our] sins, and to cleanse us from all unrighteousness.' (KJV) My very presence dispels the darkness and brings to light those things that are hidden. 'For there is nothing hidden which will not be revealed, nor has anything been kept secret but that it should come to light.' Mark 4:22 (NKJV) When My children allow My light to shine on the sin within them, that darkness dissipates and gives way to truth. This is the process through which I purify My people."

"Secrecy is a weapon of the enemy. It is a great evil in My sight. It is a tool used to convince My children that if they allow themselves to become vulnerable to one another, others will judge them. Men care more about the thoughts of other men than then they do of My judgment. Yet what I desire is that they judge the sin in their own lives and expose it for what it is, and they would be healed. If they would be obedient in this, I would not have to do it for them in such a painful way. I put them together as a family for this purpose, that they may share their flaws with one another. Since they are all equally tempted, they have no right to be harsh towards each another, and if some choose to go that route, I will deal with that as well. Yet I will also not tolerate them encouraging one another to sin. They must confess sin and call it what it is, while having the compassion that brings repentance and forgiveness. It is equally destructive to sympathize with sin or the spirit behind it. I have commanded them to walk in the light as I am in the light. How do they justify this shroud of darkness they wear?"

Kara began to weep. As the tears sparkled in the Light of His Glory, He lifted one from her eye. "Why do you weep?" continued the Voice of her Savior.

The words came out in a whisper, through the pain in her heart. "Jackie. Lord, I long to see her come to you." He did not reply. "Lord, if all this is so, should people expose the sins of others? Should they shame them openly in order to help them? And should people tell everyone about all their sins?"

"Certainly not. Love covers sin in others. And men need not tell everyone all their transgressions, for then those others would take My place as the forgiver of sin, and the weak would be caused needlessly to stumble. I have commanded that they confess before Me that they have sinned, and I promise them forgiveness in return.

At the time of forgiveness, the process of cleansing begins, in which I use many ways to remove the sin completely. Some resist the discipline, not accepting it as their friend. A certain scourging must begin, which frequently takes some time. This can become very painful if they fight against the work I am doing. There must needs be accomplished a complete repentance of all that is associated with that sin. How often must I remind them that I scourge every son I receive? Though I do require honesty, I have placed within each a certain knowing of who to confide in, if he truly wants to obey. It is not My design, however, that men live their lives separated from one another by this cloak of darkness. For how can they learn to love each other any other way? And is it not true that they hide their sins merely to save their own pride? This is foolishness, as they actually cannot hide anyway, since the One whose opinion matters already knows all about it. There comes a time when I will expose the sin myself, as you now understand, in order to bring healing. Men are hindered by dark wounds that fester into massive infections of evil, simply because they will not come to the light. Evil thrives in darkness, for it is the absence of God. There is no sin I cannot deal with once it is in the light."

The King pulled her closer into His chest as she continued to cry. She shed the tears of sorrow for Jackie and for the sin she had once condoned. And she cried for a billion people who did not understand what was lost by their refusal to embrace all that the King had to offer. Though she did not cry out, she again felt the pain from the marks within her, reminding her of earlier times, especially concerning Jackie. Kara knew she was forgiven, but she could not fully forget. Gently He stroked her face and hair, and she saw Him saving her tears in a flask. "These are holy," He whispered. "They have stood the test of true repentance and compassion." He whispered in her ear, quieting her sadness, as she fell asleep in His arms. When she awakened, her heart sang to Him:

My Friend and my God
I love You
My Friend and my God
You're always true
My Friend and my God
One thing please do
Please help me to be
A friend to You!

My Friend and my God
You understand
The winds and the waves
Are at Your command
You calm the storm
And bring me through
Please help me to be
A friend to You!

Though troubles may come
You're always there
Whatever may come
I know You care
You calm the storm
And bring me through
Please help me to be
A friend to You!

"Lord," Kara addressed her King, "I am also wondering about Aunt Jenny. Everyone is so angry with her because she committed adultery, yet Uncle Steve is still with her. Some people say that he shouldn't give her another chance, since you say that he can divorce her for what she has done. But he wants to stay with her. What do you think about that? I know it is a sin, but should we give up on people so easily? She seems to be really sorry for what she has done."

"Adultery is such a black sin!" He exclaimed. "So much damage is done, and a sacred trust is broken that can be nearly impossible to repair. Many are unable to recover a marriage tainted by this evil. Though I require that such a one be forgiven, it is up to the individual as to whether or not to stay in the relationship. Yet if a man or woman who has been wronged in this way is truly able to forgive and put it away without dissolving the marriage, that one has surely done a great thing. In this I offer great reward, as it is a portrait of My compassion painted before men. As I showed you before, sexual sin is no little thing. There is so much darkness and sin that mars the offender, as well as all who are joined to this one in present or future relationships. If you read My laments over Israel, spiritual adultery was committed against Me over and over again. This is what you and I were dealing with in your art." The reminder was painful to Kara, understanding again the gravity of these things. She listened intently as He continued. "There comes a time when the offended one can no longer endure the torment. Some humans can put away the anger against an offending partner for a time, but repeated offenses may become more painful than one can bear. The offender must repent. Yet those about the couple should retain their compassion, understanding that they too are tempted by evil. They dare not indulge in passing judgment, lest they too become ensnared by the grasp of transgression. I forgive, as you have seen, but I demand repentance. Yet when repentance has taken place, an individual needs the support of others to help in the healing process. It would be more profitable to be available to help such a one than to condemn the offender, as there is no healing in this. I did not come into the world to condemn but to give life. As I told you before, men have no right to hold accounts against others when they are so fatally flawed themselves. 'Judge not, that ye be not judged. For with what judgment ye judge, ye shall be judged: and with what measure ye mete, it shall be measured to you again. And why beholdest thou the mote that is in thy brother's eye, but considerest not the beam that is in thine own eye? Or how wilt thou say to thy brother, Let me pull out the mote out of thine eye; and, behold, a beam [is] in thine own eye? Thou hypocrite, first cast out the beam out of thine own eye; and then shalt thou see clearly to cast out the mote out of thy brother's eye.' Matthew 7:1-5 (KJV) Though I do have that right, I prefer that mercy prevail over judgment, though a day of judgment must come."

"Why do so many marriages end in divorce? Even the church is full of broken relationships. It causes people to think no relationship is sacred or special." With that, His discourse began.

"My children muse at the disarray of the Church. They ponder why so many of their marriages end in divorce and there is no distinction between believers and the world in this area. Consider this. They have become a part of a throw away society, not merely the disposal of unwanted articles but of people and relationships as well. I did not create people to be disposable nor covenants to be so easily tossed aside when they are no longer convenient. Do they not see how painstakingly persistent I am in rescuing My bride, how I so freely took Israel again to Myself when she would merely show a spark of repentance? Though she committed adultery against Me with other gods, yet I took her back. I suffered torture and death to rescue My people, was crucified among sinners and counted as a transgressor for their sakes, and only with great consternation do I see those who abuse their free will slide through the gates of Hell. Yet My people freely toss aside any relationship when it becomes difficult or inconvenient. Is it any wonder that the closest of bonds between them cannot endure troubles? My children cast aside any who bring discomfort to them, allowing even the bonds of a holy covenant to slip easily through their fingers. They do this because they see no value in those I have joined unto them. Though I died on behalf of all, suffering the anguish of a spurned lover for each fallen creature, My children see no value in others who offend them. Of this they must repent, that I may again form true and holy relationships.

Do I condemn them? No, I do not. But they condemn themselves when they refuse to repent of these things. If only they would take My hand and repent that I may restore what has been lost and strengthen those things that remain, those eternal things that are of value to Me. My children must choose to follow Me in forming relationships that are not so easily broken. They need to mend these attitudes in their hearts, and then they will see the true way to go. Each person is of infinite value to Me, as are their brothers and sisters. None should allow discord to destroy what I so greatly cherish. Is it not clear in My Word that I hate discord sown among brothers? I want them to guard their own hearts that this pattern of evil not continue. For how can My Church be cohesive unless My children chose to love one another even in troubles and disagreements? How can she be an example to the world that they might be saved? My heart cries for them to draw near to Me in this, to understanding that My creation is not expendable in My sight and that none is without value to Me. They must find the ability in Me to work out relationships with painstaking patience, diligently seeking to make all things right. Thus they will truly be joined to Me. They should be quick to mend rather than to break, to hold fast rather than to loose and destroy. For I observe what is taking place among My people, and it is an offense unto Me. It is distasteful that men can so easily discard one another when I have paid such a high price to maintain My relationship with each of them. Let the brethren join in one heart, a heart of worship and love for Me. Though they do not truly understand each other or agree on many things, it is not a time to discard their love for one another and the relationships I have formed between them."

"Kara," began the King again. "Another darkness that dwells in My earth is procrastination. It is closely akin to laziness, and it causes men untold misery. 'For He says: "In an acceptable time I have heard you, And in the day of salvation I have helped you." Behold, now is the accepted time; behold, now is the day of salvation.' 2 Corinthians 6:2 (NKJV) Men put off what I tell them to do; they delay dealing with their sin. Yet there will never be an easier time to obey than the present. The longer one waits, the more the evil root grows, winding into precious parts of his soul and strangling all life in its path. It is as a cancer, growing silently in the darkness, until the damage is beyond repair. As the Master architect of humanity, I remove those horrific stains, but a painful purging must take place. Cancer is truly a natural picture of sin, as its treatment, if successful at all, is extremely hard to endure. The medications men must use destroy both good cells and bad alike, and many contemplate whether they are willing to take the treatment at all. Though I have the perfect cure, it is not without suffering. Because of the sin of procrastination, they suffer untold misery that could have been avoided."

Kara remembered a line in a friend's poem that had always stayed with her. "Oh great Queen of procrastination, where have the sparkles gone from your eyes?" There was no life in slothfulness, no spark of joy. Even on an earthly level, procrastination was as a sickness that destroyed anyone consumed by this vice. How much more was it a tool for darkness, to thwart the growth of a spiritual man? There was no such luxury when standing before God. In His presence, sin had to be dealt with swiftly and severely. How foolish it was to avoid these dealings in a place where time could act as a buffer! In avoiding these dealings, the sin grew instead in monstrous proportions, destroying the good along with the evil, polluting all in its path.

"Kara?" started her Lord. "You have had a time of rest. But there is still work to do in your heart." In a silent ritual, He removed her beautiful robes and placed work clothes on her, what appeared as old white coveralls and an old scarf that covered her flowing hair. "We must not soil your garments," He continued. As she looked into His eyes, she saw a sorrow that told her that this would be no easy task. Amidst her fingers He placed what appeared to be cleaning supplies, a scrub brush and a bucket. Taking her hand, He led her into a very dark cavern. She could scarcely breathe for the smell of mold in this damp, black place. Filth of every sort swirled about her, hitting her in the face, and the suffocating blackness was so immense that she could not see. She wondered if He had taken her to the very entrance of Hell. "Lord," she pleaded, "what does this mean?"

He looked at her sorrowfully. "I will explain, but not yet. You must take the brush in your hand and scrub this place, as it is unclean. In the bucket is the water of My Word. You must not stop cleaning though the task is great. You will not see My face to dispel this darkness, though I will truly not leave you alone. He squeezed her hand gently, as if in farewell, and He seemed to let go. No groping could find Him, and a terror rested within her, as she felt terribly alone. Kara knew there was no way out of this darkness but to obey His command, so she lifted the brush, dipping it into the water, and began.

Placing the brush on the nearest surface, Kara scrubbed with an intensity of a thousand workmen. To her horror, every movement of the brush resulted in searing pain, for it was as if the brush was scouring her very insides. Yet she persisted, lonely for her King, cleaning for what seemed to be day upon eternal day, with no light. She did not sleep and took no comforts, but rather worked in a continuous frenzy. When she cried out for Him, there was no answer, just the echo of His voice in her mind instructing her to go on. She was sure this agony was more than she could bear, yet she persisted, night upon night of black horror, she continued on. Making it especially more difficult, she saw absolutely no results from her labors, yet she obeyed His command. As her being became raw beyond comprehension, and her tears blended with the water, she finally collapsed, crying desperately for His return. "I can't clean this!" was her agonizing cry.

"Pour out all the water in this place," came the eternal echo. "This is My Word. It is the only thing that will suffice." As she gathered a strength she was sure she did not have, she tipped the bucket. From it flowed rivers of the sparkling waters in which she had been baptized. Jewels flowed into each crevice, and sweet perfume consumed the moldy, evil darkness. "Pour out the other bucket," she heard. Looking at her side, she saw another bucket, barely visible now in the light of the flowing waters of His Word. As she reached to tip the bucket, her strength was returning. Spilling from its mouth came a mighty ocean of blood, His Blood. She gasped as she felt it enter into her as well.

Now able to see Her Lord, she noted that He was but a few inches from her. Pulling her to His breast, He proceeded to explain, as she donned her flowing robes again. "This place is where I store the idle words that men have spoken. You were not able to remove them from you, no matter how great your efforts. Only My Word can answer them, and only My blood can remove them from My sight. 'But I say to you that for every idle word men may speak, they will give account of it in the day of judgment.' Matthew 12:36 (NKJV) The tongue is such a potent weapon, for good or for evil, and men yield it without deliberation. With it they dig the very deepest of caverns, the cruelest seats of destruction, and yet with it one can draw up a balm of healing for the nations." Holding her face in His hand, He opened her mouth. On her tongue he placed a fiery, white hot coal. The pain at first was excruciating, yet He held it firmly in place, that a searing might ensue. Slowly, the pain dissipated, yet the intensity of the fire remained and actually amplified. Though she could never explain the sensation if given many words to do so, she loved the fire and all it represented. She knew His flame was upon her lips, his authority on her tongue, a blaze to purify. One Word from her mouth, His mouth, could pierce any heart and destroy the evil works of man.

"And the tongue is a fire, a world of iniquity. The tongue is so set among our members that it defiles the whole body, and sets on fire the course of nature; and it is set on fire by hell." James 3:6 (NKJV)

"Now out of His mouth goes a sharp sword, that with it He should strike the nations. And He Himself will rule them with a rod of iron. He Himself treads the winepress of the fierceness and wrath of Almighty God." Revelations 19:15 (NKJV)

Lifting her up by the hand, the King caused Kara to stand beside Him. His magnificence awed her more at every glance. "I want you to walk with Me," he started, and with no effort at all, she marched with Him as if in a mighty procession. Angels encompassed them all around. She knew they sang of His glory, proclaiming His greatness with every syllable, yet she could not understand a single word that surged forth from deep within them. Each creature had a voice, an intimate song with its Master, that no one else could comprehend. "Gaze with Me upon My creation," ensued His command. He took her to what she thought was the edge of the Earth. There were birds of every kind, flying in a fluid motion through the crystal clear morning air. Trees with leaves of every color, hues she had never before envisioned, painted themselves vividly in her mind. Flowers innumerable were cast upon extravagantly green grass. Land animals of every sort, the great large cats, majestic giraffes, bounding gentle deer, lambs, goats, fleeting squirrels, and every other creature, some she did not recognize. As

He held her hand, they flew over oceans and rivers filled with water creatures of every type. The delightful sea horse, fish in constant motion, great dolphins and whales, and again some of which she knew nothing about.

Halting over His creation, the King's Voice rang out in a mighty command. "Stand and watch what has become of these!" Horror filled Kara's heart as thick, black, smoky clouds invaded the scene. Animals and plants, creatures of every sort, died in masses before their eyes. Angry rumblings of evils and wars filled the skies, and a multitude of voices cried out in anguish, the endless cry of ages of destruction, piercing their ears. They were pleading with the King to stop their torment, to bring their sufferings to an end. There were men and women, infants and toddlers, who also cried out. "Every creature has a voice that speaks to My heart," His voice chimed. "I have a song for every creature, a joy and a lamentation of love for every woman and every man, every child and every creature that has life in it. They cry out for deliverance, for Me to bring this suffering from the evil one to an end."

"For we know that the whole creation groans and labors with birth pangs together until now. Not only that, but we also who have the firstfruits of the Spirit, even we ourselves groan within ourselves, eagerly waiting for the adoption, the redemption of our body...... Likewise the Spirit also helps in our weaknesses. For we do not know what we should pray for as we ought, but the Spirit Himself

makes intercession for us with groanings which cannot be uttered."
Romans 8:22-23,26 (NKJV)

A song came forth from deep within Kara, and she began to
sing over His creation:

Remember where He brought you from
Remember from where you have come
Remember when the day is done
Remember and return to the Lord.

Remember what He brought you through
Remember what He says He will do
Remember what He promised you
Remember and return to the Lord.

Remember how you cried out to grow
Remember, that His face He would show
Remember how you promised to go
Remember and return to the Lord.

The King stood, overlooking the Earth, and began to speak to the
hearts of men. It was not apparent if they heard with their ears, but Kara
knew the proclamation entered into the hearts of the great many who were
His. She knew that on the day of judgment, none would be able to say that
He had not spoken these things to them:

"Is this not the day of gathering? I am gathering My people from
the four corners of the earth, from the north, from the south, from
the east, from the west. My army is forming, gathering those who

have fallen and those who still stand. Many would say, 'I have heard this before. It will not come.' But I say, the Lord is not slow as some count slowness. I have not been willing that any should perish. But this is truly a time to tune in to My Voice, to hear what I have to say to you. Return to Me, come quickly. For shall the last leg of the race be less than the first? Put forth your strength, your courage to believe Me, and stretch forth the legs with which you run, lest you miss the blessings I have for you and weep for the loss that will come. I have kept your little ones and will bring them back to Me. Put forth your hand to the plow and follow Me. Do not let the harvest die on the vine. I am gathering, gathering, gathering. Make haste to gather with Me, for time is growing short even as I speak."

The sounds of drums began to rumble and a trumpet was playing, as if to proclaim a battle. As He smiled sadly, she again began to sing:

Do you hear the battle cry?
Do you hear the drums of war?
Do you hear the trumpet sound?
This is the day of our God.

Awake oh His people, rise up!
Come forth from the places where you hide!
The day of His glory is upon you!
Take up your weapons and ride!

A great rumbling was heard, as the sound of many horses, as her voice echoed in a crystal clear refrain:

Come forth you army of the Lord
Come forth now and stand
Come forth you army of the Lord
Come forth at His command.

Can you not see?
Do you not hear Him calling,
"Come forth"?

Come forth you army of the Lord
Come forth now and fight
Come forth you army of the Lord
Come forth for what is right.

Can you not see?
Do you not hear Him calling,
'Come forth'?

Gazing into His stricken eyes, Kara began a new song, crooning from deep within her. The sound was sweeter than that of many angels as she comforted her Lord.

The Spirit and the Bride say, Come.
The Spirit and the Bride say, Come.
Come, Lord Jesus.
Come, Lord Jesus.

All creation sings,
All creation calls,
Come Lord Jesus,

Come Lord Jesus.

All creation cries,
All creation groans,
Come, Lord Jesus.
Come, Lord Jesus.

Though they left that place, it was sealed forever in the heart of the
King and His princess, her head sinking deeply into His chest, where
she had stroked His very heart.

Chapter 8

David's head pounded. He usually did not suffer migraines, but the intense emotions of these past months seemed to descend upon him in a new fury. He was too ill to continue working, so he made arrangements and started home. Everything ached. His entire being had been assaulted. In his car, the humming of the engine seemed to have its own special message for the man. It was as if it were demanding an answer from him. "No room? No room? No room?" it chanted. Convinced that God was trying to tell him something, he contemplated what this could mean amidst the searing pain in his head. "What, God?" he cried, his pain exploding into a torrent of tears. "No room for what?"

In his heart, David could hear the Redeemer. "What about the boy?" He asked.

"What about him?" David snapped back. "What has he got to do with anything?"

"He is Savannah's son," the Voice persisted. "He is My son. Do you have room for My son, David?"

"I guess he can live here," he grumbled, his migraine stronger than ever.

"David," persisted His Lord. "Do you have room for My son?"

Though he would like to have accepted this question as a reference to Jesus, David knew to whom the Lord was referring. "I said he could live here. What else do you want? He is not even mine." David regretted these words the moment they escaped his lips, but there was no way of swallowing them up again.

"He is My son, David! Is that not enough?"

"So what do you want, Lord? How do I owe him anything?"

At this point he felt an anger pointed towards him. "You owe him much more than you will ever know! He stood with Savannah when you would not, and much that I have done in you and in your family has been due to his frequent supplications on your behalf! What do you owe him?"

The bitterness that had grown within him was now apparent and ugly. "So what do you want me to do? I'm sorry!"

"Are you?" his Master let that sink in. "Is that true repentance? 'Behold, thou desirest truth in the inward parts: and in the hidden [part] thou shalt make me to know wisdom.' Psalms 51:6 (KJV) Do you think you can deceive Me? You should be crying out for My mercy!" David was reeling from the words. "You ask what I desire? I want you to repent! I want you to truly forgive Jeremy! I want you to love My son!" At this point the tears were flowing. There were no vacations in the dealings of his Lord with him. It seemed that the onslaught of coping with his shortcomings would never end, and his head felt like it would explode. "David! I want you to make room for Jeremy! I want you to accept him as your son!"

Before he could stop the words, they rose up within him and passed the gate of his tongue. "Yeah, well you took my child!"

"Took, David? Took? So was it a lie when you said Kara was Mine?" the Voice nearly roared in his head, multiplying the migraine many times over. "How heavy must My hand be upon you before you obey?"

All the pent up agony of David's soul seemed to burst out in cries and screams, guttural laments for all that had transpired over these many months. Though it had seemed that the wells of despair could never expand to hold his sorrow, the cavern had grown deeper. "Forgive me, Lord!" he cried, with all the ferocity within him. "Please forgive me! I will accept the boy! I will accept Jeremy!" Then he cried out like David of old, "Create in me a clean heart, O God; and renew a right spirit within me. Cast me not away from thy presence; and take not thy holy spirit from me. Restore unto me the joy of thy salvation; and uphold me [with thy] free spirit." Psalms 51:10-12 (KJV)

"David, you must not merely accept Jeremy. You must love him as your son." David's injured heart submitted, as entering his home and locking the door behind him, he fell on the bed. The room remained dark, and he was asleep.

....

"Kara." She loved to hear Him call her name. "We have more work to do," proclaimed the King. Again He removed her robes from her and placed a set of work clothes in their place, reminding her that her robes must not be soiled. Her sadness grew,

186

knowing that what was before her would likely diminish His presence for a time. A scrub brush in hand and the buckets beside her, she followed His lead. His steps were heavy, dripping with sadness, as he led her by the hand. "This place will be exceptionally dark," He told her. "You will not be able to see Me, and you will hear Me only in your heart. You must take your brush and the buckets, and clean this place. There are no short cuts. This lesson, too, must be learned in full." He held her face in His hands, as she looked into His face, and a great sorrow filled His eyes. She smiled trustingly back, acknowledging in her motion that she would accept what had to be done. In an instant, she was falling into a black abyss. The scrub brush remaining in her hand, but she did not know where the buckets had gone. All about her she sensed the darkest of creatures, crawling in a black slime. She fell a very great distance, further and further into the blackness. As her fall came to a halt, she was not sure on what surface she lay. There was a faint glow encompassing her, and the filthy creatures that she could hear crawling about her seemed unable to reach past the glow to touch her. The odor of the place filled her nostrils with a distinct smell of decay, more offensive than any she had ever encountered. The aroma alone was enough to cause her great dismay. She deduced that it was the scent of human remains, or even something worse. Every vile thing was there, as evil thoughts were flung into her consciousness, visions of murders and torments and things infinitely horrific beyond her worst imaginations. The Voice in Kara's heart echoed. "Take the brush and clean." Kara was horrified. She could not locate the buckets. She began to cry in anguish, for the enormity of what was before her, for the lack of cleaning supplies, and for the very evilness of this place. Her tears flowed endlessly, and her heart ached for her Maker. "Use your tears," she heard Him say. "Use your tears on the brush, and begin with haste!"

Night upon eternal night, she scrubbed with all the force in her, her own tears and sorrow the only fluid to wash the walls of this abyss. Again the cleaning she attempted was scouring her heart as well. There was no scarcity of tears, as she was filled with the mourning of the ages. The blackness and stench were suffocating, yet she continued on. She neither slept nor ate but continued to bathe the place with her despairing tears, and still the job went on. Again there seemed no progress, as her tortured heart broke to be with her Lord. The growing pain within her intensified with each stroke, and yet she worked on. She called for Him but heard nothing, deepening her distress. Though her strength seemed to be failing, she was compelled to persist in her efforts. The crawling creatures seemed to multiply about her, refusing to die, and the slime and mold flourished. There was no end to this black place where she had been made to dwell. Yet in her feebleness, she scrubbed on. This place was infinitely more evil than anywhere she had been or could remotely imagine. Finally collapsing, she cried out again. "Lord, I cannot go on!"

In her heart she heard His Voice. "Take the buckets as before." In an instant, they were setting beside her. "Pour forth the blood first," He commanded. As she tipped the pail, oceans upon oceans of blood flowed into the abyss. Reaching for the other container, she released the rivers of His Word. They flowed endlessly throughout the darkness, and many of the creatures scampered this way and that. Even the jewels in the water seemed a torment to these creatures. Yet the blackness and evil remained. "Open your mouth" she heard from within her. Though terror tried to taunt her, providing visions of the creatures crawling into her mouth and throat, entering into her very being, she knew she must obey His Voice. Evil jeered, proclaiming that the Voice within her was not His at all but merely her own contrived thoughts. Yet the child knew His Voice and could not be deceived by the lies amidst this darkness.

As Kara opened her mouth, a mighty Fire came forth, the Fire of her baptism in His Spirit. It consumed the creatures as they were screaming, trying in vain to escape and scurry away, and the fire enveloping her as well. The walls became white hot in fury against the darkness, and she felt a pulling on her being. She was being lifted from the abyss, back to her Saviors arms. Again He placed her robes upon her, as she leaned against His chest. Though it would seem her tears were used up, yet they flowed in a torrent from her. He stroked her head, comforting her and giving her wounded heart rest. Her despairing cries went on into that eternal night, refusing to be consoled, until He touched her weary soul with His hand. Though the agony remained, it seemed to subside a bit.

"Kara," He began gently, "the evil of that place is great before Me. It is the abyss where the secrets of the hearts of men are stored. There dwells every murderous imagination and deceit of every sort. There men justify all that is evil and nurture their wickedness. Buried in the blackness are many hideous crimes. The blood of the innocent has been shed there, and men care nothing for these cries. They think I should allow this darkness into My very presence, yet it must be consumed by My Fire. Hell itself is no deeper than their treachery, and I will not abide with their lies." Her crushed heart gave off a sweet aroma in His nostrils, as of many compressed precious flowers and spices formed into a holy perfume; all the while she lay upon His chest weeping, until He covered Her in sleep. Amidst a holy dream, she softly sang to her Love, comforting Him of the evil He had to abide:

> May I be a resting place
> May I be a resting place
> When Your Spirit hovers o'er the earth
> May I be a resting place
>
> When Noah sent the dove from the ark
> Over a world once so dark
> She found no place for her feet
> And returned back into the ark again

May I be a resting place
May I be a resting place
When Your Spirit hovers o'er the earth
May I be a resting place

When Noah sent the dove out again
Over a world once filled with sin
She found a twig of new life
And returned back into the ark again

May I be a resting place
May I be a resting place
When Your Spirit hovers o'er the earth
May I be a resting place

When Noah sent the dove one last time
Over a world now sublime
She found a place for her feet
And returned not into the ark again

May I be a resting place
May I be a resting place
When Your Spirit hovers o'er the earth
May I be a resting place

"The heart is deceitful above all things, And desperately wicked; Who can know it?" Jeremiah 17:9 (NKJV)

"For His anger is but for a moment, His favor is for life; Weeping may endure for a night,
But joy comes in the morning." Psalms 30:5 (NKJV)

....

"Kara," began the King. I have more to show you." The celestial beings looked on, marveling at her beauty as she looked up into His face. Her countenance reflected His very Light. "Let us walk a bit from here." She was taken to a very high place, overlooking a large building. It appeared to have been a marvelous, ornate building at one time with precious gems and much pure gold; but it was in very poor condition. It reminded her of pictures depicting Solomon's temple in the Old Testament.

"My temple is in ruins," He began.

"Can You send workers to fix it?" Kara asked.

"This is but a picture of My true temple," He continued. "Look and see."

Below her was a huge number of people. They were fighting, some with swords and weapons, some with fists, and some fired arrows from their mouths. Many were bleeding and dying. There seemed to be total confusion, and it was impossible to ascertain what was actually going on. There were no clear boundaries defining friend or foe, though some congregated in groups to fight against others.

"What does this mean, Lord?" Kara asked quizzically. "Who are these, and what are they doing?" As she waited, she heard a proclamation from the heavens above them:

"Is this not the day to repair My temple? You are My temple; you are the temple of God. Yet the world has seen a temple in ruins. They have seen you broken down. They have seen your flaws. I have called you to repair the temple, not one man or one woman, lest the job be too much. I have called each to repair the wall in his own house, and then to help those who cannot do the work. Repent in the areas you know to repent. Lay aside the sins you know of in your lives, each to his own area. Even as the world saw My Son Jesus on the cross and disdained His humanity, they have looked upon you in your death and have mocked. Yet I am preparing to present My bride in her resurrection, even as My Son was presented in His resurrection. They will look once more at a holy and purified church, that My Name may be proclaimed. Then shall they run to Me. Then shall they cry out. Blessed be those who have shared in My death even as in My resurrection. Allow Me to heal you that the world may experience My glory and call on My Name."

"These are My people, My Church, My Temple where I want to dwell," the Lord explained. "They are My children who have gathered against each other. Many do not even know why they quarrel but merely that they are not at ease with the other. I have instructed them to love one another. I have told them that they are My temple: 'Or do you not know that your body is the temple of the Holy Spirit who is in you, whom you have from God, and you are not your own?' 1 Corinthians 6:19 (NKJV) Yet they have not heard. It is time for them to shore up the gaps, each in his own place, as in the time of Nehemiah and Ezra. They are each so concerned with the faults of others that they do not seek Me to teach them how to repair their own areas, the place each one lives, which is the sphere of responsibility of each man or woman. If they would do this, afterwards they could help the few that still needed assistance. Instead, they fight and destroy the temple further, and they ignore the instructions I have given them to fix what they can."

"Lord, shall I go and speak with them?" asked Kara, seeing the distress on His face. He nodded, and she donned the robes of mankind and mingled among them. Kara spoke the words of her Lord, expecting that they would be pleased to know the truth. Yet instead many of them became angry. They cast darts with their mouths and beat her until she lay bleeding, crying to the King to rescue her. A few of them tried to help her, but they were outnumbered, and many of those who helped her were beaten as well. Snatching her from them, He cleaned her wounds and restored her robes as she cried on His chest. She saw His anger, though mixed with compassion, lighting upon His face as He comforted her.

"So they do as they have always done, rejecting those I send! '…….. There was a certain landowner who planted a vineyard and set a hedge around it, dug a winepress in it and built a tower. And he leased it to vinedressers and went into a far country. Now when vintage-time drew near, he sent his servants to the vinedressers, that they might receive its fruit. And the vinedressers took his servants, beat one, killed one, and stoned another. Again he sent other servants, more than the first, and they did likewise to them. Then last of all he sent his son to them, saying, "They will respect my son." But when the vinedressers saw the son, they said among themselves, "This is the heir. Come, let us kill him and seize his inheritance." So they took him and cast him out of the vineyard and killed him. Therefore, when the owner of the vineyard comes, what will he do to those vinedressers?' Matthew 21:33b-40 (NKJV) When I went Myself, they did as this parable states. And now it continues in My Church, My body, My very possession. How shall I answer this?"

Kara rested quietly without reply. This was indeed a great darkness that had fallen upon the Earth. His words echoed in her thoughts. "For the time has come for judgment to begin at the house of God; and if it begins with us first, what will be the end of those who do not obey the gospel of God? Now 'If the righteous one is scarcely saved,

Where will the ungodly and the sinner appear?' Therefore let those who suffer according to the will of God commit their souls to Him in doing good, as to a faithful Creator."
1 Peter 4:17-18 (NKJV)

Though He saw their rebellion, He continued to call unto His people. He was wooing them, calling them to come together to become His bride. His Voice resounded with the pain of One rejected, yet He continued for the few that would hear. While the Earth grew darker with wickedness, there was thunder and lightening in the heavens, and a great fire formed among them as He continued His refrain:

"Do you understand that I am about to shake the darkness? Even now it has already begun. Do not hang on to the things of this world, for they are not steady. They are about to crumble even between your fingers, and only that which is of Me shall remain. Set your gaze on me, and I will steady your path. For even the ground beneath you shall quake and tremble before Me. None shall be immune to My judgment as I set one against another, daughter against mother, son against father, and as I have spoken, "...'a man's enemies will be those of his own household." (Mathew 10:36) This is a time to set aside your own opinions and preferences, your own ideas about Me, about Who I Am, and Who you want Me to be. I Am Who I Am, and I do not change with your whims and opinions. Trust Me and believe that I Am right, the only Righteous One, and there is no other. I will share My glory with no other gods, as I Am the Eternal One. All others are the creation of another, but I created all things. Do not attempt to conform Me into your image or to fit Me into your conceptions of what I should Be. For of a truth, who are you who answers back to God and complains against Him in His designs? (Romans 9:20-21) Be transformed instead into My image. (Romans 12:2) If you would be steady in your walk, hold tight to My hand, for in Me alone are you secure. Put aside all relationships that hinder your walk, and give them all to Me. Come and follow Me, and I will truly give you rest. Then will you see My deliverance, both for you and your loved ones. Be of those who can truly say with Me, "... for the prince of this world cometh, and hath nothing in me." (John 14:30b KJV)"

At this many trembled, afraid for the things coming upon them. Yet He steadied their hands and their hearts and spoke kindly to them. His heart longed for them to respond to His proclamations, that they would lavish the love and worship upon Him that was a consummation of their relationship together, that which He had placed in their hearts to give. Yet His Voice continued:

"Why is it that My people tremble at the approaching darkness even as the world trembles? Do they not understand that I AM made known in the darkness? Do they not know that where sin abounds, grace much more abounds? My pillar of fire is greatly apparent when men are in darkness, groping to see even their hands in front of their faces. This is the time to rejoice in knowing that I will be revealed among the nations. Though you are to continue to seek Me and My deliverance for your nations, do not be dismayed at the darkness. As you show forth My glory in the darkness, many will come to know Me. I want to unite My Church in holiness and in love. When this takes place and you join together, you will be as a pillar of fire in the darkness. You will illuminate the places where you walk and dwell. It is time to lay aside your petty differences and to call on My name together. I love My Church. Though you see her flaws, do not forsake her. Rather bring her healing, bring her My love that she may be restored to her true glory. I am her glory, and she is My glory. Do not attempt to separate Us, for the day will come when you will see Us truly as One. Do not be numbered among those who attack her, lest you be found attacking yourselves, and even Me, as well. Trust Me in all this and you will see what I will do."

Kara was struck by the awe of it all. She saw a few among the group coming together, washing their robes in a tub of blood, His blood. When they drew out the garments, they were pure white, sparkling in appearance. "I will have a Church, Kara, that is clean," He proclaimed. Many of the others that still refused to join them fell in battle and were absorbed into the Earth out of her sight. "The time has come, Kara, for My people to make a choice. The battle against evil has already begun. Some have chosen to be absorbed again into the evil ways of this world, but these in white are preparing for battle against the evil one, rescuing all that would follow them away from the darkness and even raising those who have fallen."

At this point a storm began to form, a light rain that grew heavier each moment. The people in its path became very afraid. They cried out as their possessions were swept away with the waters, fearing for their very lives as well. Yet as she watched them struggle, some swam and others groped for safety, but none perished. The people around them which were not of their group clung to them for help, and they were rescued as well. He again spoke over His people:

"Do you feel My rain descending upon you? Bask in My presence. Yet listen closely as you hear the rumbling, the thunder of My voice, as the rain becomes heavier, even a torrent. Do not be afraid, for this storm is of Me. I will bring heavy waters to wash you clean, to remove those things in your lives that are not of Me. Do not cling to those things but hold fast to Me. Hold fast lest the flood waters overtake you and you be washed away. Yet understand My mercy as I keep you alive, and you will remain standing when the storm subsides. Am I not even able to make you stand? Thus you will be a beacon amidst the waters, a lighthouse of refuge for those who do not know Me. Look and marvel how so much can be destroyed and washed away, yet the loss of life be limited to none. Am I not a great and glorious God, amazing and terrible among the people? Let your feet stand firmly on the Rock, for I am your Rock and your Salvation."

Many were sorrowful, weeping for their losses, and He comforted them. A few were very tired, and He carried them away from the Earth. Many that remained also mourned for those that were taken, wailing with a great lament. Yet He reached out His hand over them with comfort and spoke kindly to them again:

"Is this not a day of rejoicing? But you have made it a day to mourn. It is not a day to rejoice because all the circumstances are in your favor, but rather it is a day to rejoice in the Lord, for the joy of the Lord is your strength in tribulation. I do not say that all will appear well or that you will not suffer. For in your suffering you can become more like Me. Hold tight to My hand, and I will draw you nearer to Me. If a woman can be healed by touching the hem of My garment, what will become of those who hold My hand? For I would do great things among you, great things in the midst of your suffering and loss. In your loss and suffering, you will find gain. All that is lost will be gain to you, and all will be restored in its time. Only hold fast to Me, lest you fall into temptation during this time. What you give to Me, I can keep. What is mine is under My protection. Be quick to relinquish that which you have clutched tightly, for only in Me is anything secure or safe. Is this not a day of rejoicing? For each day you are a day closer to joining Me for eternity. Rejoice, for your redemption draws near, even at the door. But you must walk through this darkness, experience this death, as you walk into My arms forever. Purpose to be among those who hear Me say, 'Well done, good and faithful servant! Enter into the joy of your Lord!' Rejoice with those who have passed into My presence, knowing that one day you will join them. Though you are right to have sorrow, let your sorrow be seasoned with joy. Dance before Me, for this is a day of great joy!"

Kara watched as they began to hear His Voice and be comforted. There was a great celebration that ensued, with much dancing and singing, and there was a great feast. They lifted their voices in proclamation of His greatness, and a great fire burned over them, both purifying them and proclaiming the holiness of the King. Their voices blended as one, and their singing took on a celestial quality. Kara saw the face of her Lord as He donned a majestic smile, tears of rapture flowing down His cheeks. "This is the sacrifice of praise, and it shall rise up in glory before Me. This is their love song, singing as one to Me."

Resting her head deep against His heart, Kara fell fast asleep. In this state, she began dreaming. She was inside an old, stark castle.

There were no furnishings anywhere, just dark old cement. She saw a young girl, very plain in appearance. There were attendants in the castle, gathering women into another room for beautification, preparing them to be presented before the King. The young girl stood waiting in the unfurnished area, and something was supernaturally conveyed upon her. It was a spiritual impartation, as the power of God overcame her and overwhelmed her. As she sunk to the floor, a fire enveloped her. Kara knew that something spectacular had taken place, and that the girl could never again be the same, as a mark of power had been placed upon her. Kara noted that the girl was being made into a princess, reminding her of the Cinderella story. She was ushered into a room where others were also being prepared with beauty treatments, perfumes and oils, and every kind of extravagance. The attendants worked extensively on the other women, taking so long with this process for them that they had barely started with the young girl when the king made His entrance into the room, as it was time for whatever was about to take place. He stood there, and Kara questioned whether He would wait or say that she should come without this care. In the dream, she received no answer to the dilemma.

Kara awakened in the arms of Jesus, a dire question in her heart. What did this mean, and why was the girl not fully prepared? Jesus smiled at her, knowing the vision He had placed within her. "Kara," He began. "Are you troubled by the dream?"

"Yes Lord," she answered, the disturbance growing, "Who was the girl, and what does it mean? Why weren't her preparations complete? Will she be waited for?"

"Kara," He began. "The girl is My Church. Though she is not very attractive to the world, she has been chosen to be given to Me. I have sent many to help prepare her, but they have become so enthralled by other things that they have neglected her. Some are captivated by the other beautiful beings in My castle, and they nourish them rather than My bride. The very gifts I have given to them to help her, to bring about her purification and beautification, are themselves nourished instead. They have taken these gifts to themselves, to revel in them and to take pride in them, and these have not been properly bestowed upon my destitute bride. They toy with the very tools I have given them, building shrines to their own credit, and ignoring the most precious work of all. The time is upon them, to present her for Me."

"But will You wait?" she persisted, perplexed by the vision.

"Some things are not to be revealed yet," He responded. "But if she is not prepared as I desire, who shall I charge for these things? Who is responsible?"

It was a question she knew was not hers to answer, except to hold it in her heart. Yet she ached within her for the knowledge of what He had spoken. Her head against His breast, she was becoming ever more joined to His heart. In His comfort, she fell asleep.

....

David stared at the body of his daughter. Though her petite chest moved up and down with the rhythm of the respirator, there were no signs of spontaneous life in her. Her brown, wavy hair had grown back to a normal length in the nine months since the accident, though nearly every part of her flesh was scarred by the cuts and burns of the accident. Savannah seemed to have somehow finally found a peace in these happenings, though the sorrow was obviously still there. But David felt he had been left without comfort. A part of him was angry that Savannah seemed to have found solace in Jeremy's presence, as he was unwilling to allow the boy to replace Kara in his own heart. Though deep inside he knew Savannah would never truly allow this either, he could not help but feel a bit of resentment at the thought. Magnifying his emotions, he was less than thrilled at allowing Jeremy a place in his own heart. He knew what he had to do, but everything in him rebelled at the though of accepting the son of another man, one with whom Savannah had once had sexual relations with, as his own child. Everything in him screamed that God was requiring too much, and he had yet to tell Savannah and Jeremy what he had been instructed to do. All he wanted right now was for Kara to return to him and for Jeremy to disappear from his life forever. His suffering was heightened by the knowledge that the machines would be turned off in two days, and though it seemed futile to even wait that long, he could not bear to subtract even one moment as Kara lay before him. David angrily pushed his tears away as Savannah entered the room with Jeremy in tow. How dare this boy intrude upon his sorrow! He was not accustomed to others observing his tears, and he was especially displeased that Jeremy had been the one to see them.

"David," Savannah began gently, "we need to talk." Annoyed by the statement, David looked away from her, gazing at Kara's form. Couldn't she even wait for a break in his grief to do this? Jeremy stepped out of the room, sensing it was an awkward time for his presence, and excused himself to get a snack. Once he was out of the room, the conversation began. "David," she began again, "Jeremy is losing his apartment." She hesitated. "He lost his job a month ago."

David wanted so intensely to make some quip about the boy's character, but he knew he must not. "I suppose you want him to stay with us," he grumbled, still not looking at her. "He can have the guest room I suppose." He faltered as he persisted in his speech, then continued emphatically. "He is not getting Kara's room. That's where I draw the line."

Savannah walked down to the vending area to tell her son the news, leaving David with a heart prickled by conviction. Though he had consented in his dealings with God, living it out was another matter. The tug at his heart made it clear that he must deal with this quickly and according to God's plan, but his mind was throwing a temper tantrum. Reaching out his hand, David held Kara's fingers between his, stroking her skin. If only he could hold her again, maybe this torment would be gone. He touched her face, pushing her hair away from those beautiful eyes now closed in eternal sleep, longing to hold his playful little girl again. It overwhelmed him to think about the many times he had sent her away when she interrupted his busy life. Busy with what? It all seemed so senseless now.

As Savannah and Jeremy returned, David knew he had to make a move. The syllables came more easily than he imagined as he reached out his hand to Jeremy. His mouth opened, and his stream of words brought healing to both men. "Welcome to the family, son." David was taken back at first as the boy embraced him and started to sob. His cries were soon blended with David's own tears, and a joining of hearts took place. David marveled at God's provision. God had formed in the man what He had required of him. "If you want," David began softly, choking with emotion, "you can call me Dad. You can have Kara's room." Though Jeremy declined the offer of his sister's quarters, something magnificent had taken place. Savannah joined in tearfully, overjoyed at what God had done. For a few seconds, all three actually forgot their pain. Perhaps Kara had given him her parents, Jeremy thought, still reeling from the loss of the couple who had adopted him. And perhaps he could help David and Savannah through the loss of Kara. The three found places at Kara's beside, determined to fulfill the last two days of their waiting vigil together as a family, taking turns getting food for each other when it was needed. What an amazing thing God had done through the loss of this precious child!

....

Kara was in absolute ecstasy as she was awakened to the kiss of her Lord upon her cheek. She was fully enthralled in His presence, loving everything about Him. She was even beginning to memorize many of the features of His face, though it was so glorious that the facets of its beauty were endless and varied. Even the thought of Him was enough to swallow up the breath within her. Yet she began to feel unsettled, remembering that she had been in another dream. In the dream, she saw a woman walking in a dark place, like a small town. There were street lamps lighting the walkways. The woman was hiding a small boy under her shirt, acutely aware of a need to avoid a certain evil that was following her and to protect the child.. At some point, the woman was seated in a bright room, artificially lit with a intense light. She was sitting before her enemy, the child occasionally being exposed briefly. It was as though the enemy caught glimpses of the boy but was unsure of whether or not his eyes were deceiving him. When the child was fully revealed, however, there were many others around, and it was too late for him to destroy the boy. The woman danced with the boy in the streets, accompanied by many other children who took safety in her presence. The enemy observed all this and was wroth, vowing to destroy her. She had become the salvation of these children, and he was furious. The woman made haste, entering a tan colored jeep that had no roof. She became disturbed, as she thought she had left her purse in the place from which she had escaped, and returning for some supplies, determined to obtain it. Her purse contained her credit cards. Fleeing to the vehicle without finding the purse, she had another girl in the vehicle, presumably her daughter, who asked her what she would do without the credit cards, but on closer inspection, she found that her purse had been in the vehicle all along. There was not much time, so she made her escape in the vehicle. "Do you marvel at the dream?" spoke Her Savior's pure Voice, rippling in a way that the most peaceful of bubbling streams must have copied, penetrated her very being.

"Yes, Lord. It troubles me."

"My servants carry precious cargo, even My very Self, to be given to the nations. Though there are fleeting glances, as the gifts within them are occasionally exposed, much has been hidden. The enemy waits to devour their precious gifts, the very life of Christ within them given to deliver all people. Yet with only glimpses of what I am doing, He is unable to do so. When all is fully exposed, he cannot do as He pleases, but in his anger, he looks for an opportunity to destroy the work and My very life within My servants. The woman seeking her purse is depending on worldly provision, yet My provision has been there all the while. The time she wastes looking is precious, as she must flee from what is designed against her. She flees in a vehicle I have prepared, uncovered by man, as I alone protect her. Thus you see no roof."

"Is that all?" asked Kara, still not fully satisfied.

Smiling at her, He responded, "That is never all, Kara. Your understanding is limited. But it is enough for now. It is enough for My bride to make herself ready, to love My appearing, and to occupy the earth until I come. It is enough if she learn to trust My provision and be faithful in what I have given her to do. It is enough if she learns to love." Kara began to cry, not understanding what the tears were even for. There was an agony in her being that came from Her Lord, as she lay upon His chest, still touching His heart. "If they would only do what I have already commanded," He whispered, "if they would merely follow My instructions, if they would just trust Me, if they would love and not devour one another." The torment of the words exploded within her like a million pieces of flaming glass, causing an acute misery to envelop her. She felt the anguish was more than she could swallow. Yet she drank deeply, wanting nothing more than to be joined completely with her Lord. The magnitude of His suffering was so great, however, that she felt she could not survive the mass of compassion and emotions. "Kara," He started, articulating her pain, "you cannot partake so deeply of My sorrow, for you are small and cannot contain it." Lifting her head in His hands, He comforted her, and though the anguish subsided, it did not go away. She clung to what remained of it, not willing to lack even this in their oneness, and He caught her tears with His Hand. "Kara," He continued gently, "you have given great comfort to Me." She smiled into His face, overjoyed to share in His pain along with His rapture. This was her Love, and she would lose nothing of the intimacy He offered her. She grasped the eternal moments, hoping none of this would ever end.

"Kara," He started in a quietness that captured the attention of every cell within her. "Do you miss your art?"

"No, Lord," she responded, and they both knew it was true. "All the art I ever did or even imagined is pitiful compared with You." She paused. "After seeing Your art and what You have made, that could give me no pleasure at all."

He smiled again, holding her closely against His heart. "I love you," He whispered, the syllables resounding with an everlasting chime within her that shook every portion of her being with its ecstasy. "You truly are Mine, and I am yours." Kara was enveloped in such delight that she was sure she would be entirely consumed by it. She could not possibly give enough back to match this bliss. "Kara," her Lord spoke. "Do you mean My creation, the display of My creatures before the fall, when you speak of My art? There is something else I would like to show you." He seemed especially excited by the prospect of what He was about to share. "Do you want to see My masterpiece?"

At this Kara was awed beyond comprehension. The King of all creation, author of all that ever was and all that ever would be, her most sacred precious Love, was choosing to allow her to look upon His masterpiece. He would allow her to see what He had painted with His very heart! She could scarcely form her rapturous words to respond. "Oh yes, Lord! Please!" He took her into His arms with a motion that made her consider that she was of infinite value to Him. They soared over the Earth, and He pointed first to a very poor place where a small dirty child sat, gleefully proclaiming that though she was not finished, she was an exquisite example of His workmanship. He pulled Kara within Himself, behind His eyes, and she gasped at the beauty she saw there. This amazing creature, though encrusted in an old clay vessel, was costly and intimately of great value. As they flew, He showed her another and another, endless pieces of His craftsmanship, each hidden in these lumps of clay. Then He took her over a church she had been before, where there were a handful of people worshipping Him. She mused as she saw the many people she had distained in her lifetime, the people in what she considered to be dry churches where she had attended as well as those with more vigor and life. Each, He would say, was quite precious, though unfinished, as these works took time, and often the clay was unyielding. "These will one day constitute My Bride," He beamed. Looking through His eyes, these held a magnificence exceeding her wildest expectations.

"Now close your eyes, Kara," He whispered. "I want to show you something absolutely incredible!" Her very being quivered with His excitement as He took her, eyes closed, to another place. "Now open them!" He seemed to nearly burst with anticipation. As she opened her eyes, Kara found herself in a most ornate room. The artistry was so superb that it captivated all her attention. Each wall was etched with the most delicate depictions. The designs woven into the texture, each deeply engraved in the most exquisite pure gold and silver lines and formations, produced a beauty and majesty that would cause any royal creature to faint in its presence. Kara was overwhelmed, as His very image was carved into those lines. She could not contain her tears as He took her from room to room, peering at His workmanship. Truly this was the greatest masterpiece of all! She continued to weep as He showed her more and more. Some rooms brought rapturous joy, some incredible pain, and each was a part of Him.

"What is this place?" she gasped, unaware that the answer would send her into a torrent of emotions and rapturous ecstasy from which she could never recover. "What is this holy shrine You have shown me?"

"Kara," He started, as though barely able to contain Himself. "These are the linings of your heart. All the work that I have done is embossed here. Each lash you received has formed a beautiful eternal mark, each singing its own tale in honor of Me, gloriously engraving those things we have experienced together. The lashes were the engraving tools that formed this majesty on the borders of your heart. They have formed My very being within you, causing these incredible designs." Then He whispered in her ear, calling her by a very special, private name that He bestowed upon her. This was her new name, known to the two of them alone. This was the name that marked their oneness and eternal intimacy. As He took her hand in His, the ring upon her finger glowed like a flame, and He led her into one last room. Nothing was written on the walls there. It was merely a smooth, dark surface. She started to weep at the sight, but He placed His finger upon Her lips. "This, Kara, is the place in your heart where we will become completely one. It is not finished yet. This is where we will find our most profound intimacy together." Kara was in such astonishment she could neither speak nor cry, nor even express any emotion at all. She simply clung to His presence, waiting for what would be.

....

David, Savannah, and Jeremy stood silently by Kara's bed, waiting for medical personnel to arrive. Their hearts were heavy and filled with dread. They knew the time was approaching Kara's very last hour, and though they had tried to prepare themselves, nothing was enough. David stroked the child's hair as Savannah held her hand, and Jeremy watched in awe of the sister he had never fully known. None spoke.

As the staff walked in, none turned to greet them or observe their countenances. "Do you want to leave while we do this?" a gentleman asked quietly. All three shook their heads. It seemed so quick as they turned off the machines, and Kara's lifeless body lay still and ashen before them. Barely able to breath, Savannah was sure they had snuffed out her own life as well. Nine months of torment were all enveloped in that one moment in time, that one flip of a switch that ended Kara's life forever. The three barely moved, sensing a profound death in the place, and it seemed their tears were used up.

After a little while, the three were asked to leave while the staff prepared Kara's body for the morgue. They were told they could look at her again after the tubes were removed and she was cleaned up. It was another insult to their hearts, as they sat grieving in a small hospital chapel. Savannah could hear the nurses laughing and talking among themselves, seemingly untouched by the entire ordeal. She heard them joking about having a nursing student prepare the body, "allowing" this student to practice "postmortem care". She wanted to scream at their apparent lack of respect but held her tongue instead. How could they possibly understand the value of her little girl, lying in that tiny marred body? She chose instead to lean back in the chair, ignoring their comments, and cry.

....

Calling Kara by her new name, the King began to speak kindly to her again. "I have one last very dark place for you to go, to complete the work I have begun. You will not be able to see My face for a time, and you will hear My voice only in your heart. This place is full of wickedness and woe, but when your eyes adjust to the darkness, you will be able to see. Though you take My gifts with you, they will not be visible to your eyes. This will be a time of great suffering, as even My presence will seem far away. Yet I will never leave you."

"Oh Lord, I will miss You so. I love hearing Your voice and looking into Your eyes." As she leaned against His chest and felt the beat of His heart, she felt His sorrow as well. She looked up at Him, smiling bravely through her tears. "I will go."

The King whispered into her heart what He was about to do. "There is one special gift you may take with you." He presented many things before her from which to chose. He showed her riches, offered her notoriety, and presented the choice of the friendship of men. Refusing them all, she made a single request, and it pleased Him greatly. Reaching out His hands, He handed her the stripes she had been given, the very lashes of correction that she had borne. "You have chosen wisely, as did Solomon of old. These will go with you in their crude state, and you will feel their pain again, but they will serve you well and protect you from sin." Silently she accepted them, knowing that they would be of immeasurable value to her as she completed her tasks and that they would remind her of His love in this very dark place. She received them with joy, understanding that they were her very salvation.

Again He whispered more in her ears, disclosing the secrets of His immediate plan that even the celestial beings did not yet know. "But Lord," she chided, nearly laughing at His words, "she'll never want to be a nurse again!"

With a glint in His eye and a playful expression, her King replied in a whispered tone, as if telling her a secret, "I never called her to be one anyway. Her mother has been talking to Me about her for a long time. This should do the job nicely." Then, as if toying with her, He continued, "Besides, I have a lot of prayers to answer." Pausing, as if to restrain His own merriment, He said, "If I were One to make a wager, which you know I need not do, I would say that by this time tomorrow, everyone in that hospital will be talking to Me!" At this she burst into full laughter. Before she was midway into the merriment, she was falling into this new abyss. Leave it to Him, she thought, to send her away laughing to stave off the tears of their parting.

Kara was sinking into a deep darkness. She sensed dark creatures all about her, and the smell of blood and terrible chemicals encompassed her. Still falling, her eyes slowly began to adjust to the darkness, and she felt as though she had been dropped into a tub of sharp pieces of glass, cutting at her flesh. The stripes began to take on a fury of torment, yet in these she took comfort. As her Lord had told her, they would be her protection from the blackness of sin about her. Her descent slowed to a stop, and it seemed as though invisible hands were rubbing the glass into her flesh. The pain was so intense that she tried to pull away. As she began to resist, her actions were followed by intense screams and the profound confusion of many voices.

Savannah jumped from her seat. Now she was really angry. The nursing student sent to prepare Kara's body had just come out of the room screaming. The disrespect was more than she could swallow. David followed, hoping to calm his wife, and Jeremy came with them besides. As they entered the room, there were many voices, and confusion was the prevalent mood of the moment. Rushing over to the body, Savannah arrived just in time to hear the word she needed so badly. Hoarsely escaping past the strictures in her throat, Kara was calling to her. "Mama!" called the flailing child. None dared to touch her, and they quickly exited the room as Savannah held the girl, crying. Color returned to Kara's face, and warmth was in her body. She was breathing on her own. David and

Jeremy were absolutely stunned and found a place to sit and recover. They could not yet process the miracle.

Chapter 9

Newspaper reporters crowded into the hospital, though staff guarded Kara's room. They flashed pictures every time the door opened and questioned nearly everyone in sight. Though Kara was breathing, she had not been awake since she first called to her mother. Staff was puzzled as to how to handle the dilemma, not sure what kind to care to provide for the child. All machinery, IV's, and feeding tubes had been removed before the child woke up. It had been twelve hours since Kara had stirred, and Savannah remained at Kara's side, waiting for any further signs of life. "Mama," Kara's hoarse voice began, startling Savannah again. "Mama, I'm back."

"I'm here," Savannah whispered, her voice quivering, as she held Kara's hand. Savannah thought it looked like the child was in a lot of pain. "I can get the nurses to give you some medicine for the pain if you want." She was able to get a few chips of ice in Kara's mouth, which resulted in intensifying the raging flames in her throat.

Kara squeaked out her objections before Savannah reached the door. "No pain medicine, Mama." Tears filled Savannah's eyes. Kara hadn't called her Mama since she was very little, and now she used the term freely. She hesitated to go get David, not wanting to leave the child alone at the hands of hospital staff and afraid to miss even a moment of this time with her daughter. Life was so very fragile and unpredictable. She felt a bit guilty leaving David out of this moment but was afraid it would disappear as quickly as it had begun. Kara refused her offer of more ice chips, afraid that if she reacted to the resulting pain, Savannah would insist on getting medicine to take it away. Kara found comfort in the agony, though she did not fully remember why. Savannah began to think sadly about the scars covering Kara's body, wondering how her child would adjust to them. Some of the marks might be able to be helped by plastic surgery, but many would always remain. As if reading her thoughts, Kara asked, "What do I look like?" Sensing Savannah's hesitation, she proceeded. "It's ok, Mama. I just want to see." Reluctantly, Savannah produced a mirror. As Kara looked at her broken form, she began to cry. Savannah need not have been concerned, however, as she could not comprehend that these were tears of joy, as Kara began to remember His gift to her. He had allowed her to carry back her stripes. Though each breath she drew sent flaming darts into her chest, she knew she was His. Looking down at her hand where His ring had been, she saw a huge scar completely around the finger where it had been severed in the accident and reattached.

"We can try some plastic surgery to remove some of it," Savannah began. She was totally unprepared for Kara's speedy response as it nearly shot from her lips.

"No! These scars are mine!" Kara seemed to relax a bit again. Then she began softly, knowing an agony deeper than physical wounds, "I miss Him so much!" At this point she decided to hide the torment, though she still felt as though she was resting in a bed of broken glass. She was keenly aware that she could never communicate all that had transpired, and felt it better not to try. Some details were a bit foggy anyway in this dark place, where even the air about her was clothed with evil. Yes, those lashes were a comfort to her, a connection to what had been, and a reminder of the sinister nature of sin. She loved them as though they were still the shining gems she knew before. Another torment gripped her as well, the nagging of this darkness telling her that it had all simply been a dream, a mere fancy of the mind, and that she had not seen her Lord at all. Though she did not believe these declarations, they continued to haunt her being incessantly. She determined that these things were too precious to flaunt before men and hid them in her heart.

Savannah was sure that Kara was referring to the boy she had been with the night of the accident, convinced that it was Daniel that she missed. She wondered what kind of therapy this would require, as the child was already punishing herself for being the one left alive. But how did she even know Daniel had died? Savannah remained silent, not sure of the wisdom of probing into her daughter's thoughts but intently wondering about their contents. She was so intensely thinking on these things that she did not hear David and Jeremy walk into the room.

Looking into his daughter's open eyes, David's broken speech came in a whisper. "Hi, Angel! We sure have missed you!" He reached over to hold his daughter, not knowing that his very touch sent jolts of lightening pain throughout her being. Kara managed to refrain her inward screams, and though she recoiled a bit, David mainly saw her faint smile. Jeremy was rapidly at her

220

bedside as well, but he seemed to sense that a lighter touch was in order as he touched her hand.

"Hey," his hushed voice started. "Glad you're back. I felt pretty jipped not getting to know my little sister." Kara smiled at him as he gave an inward sigh of relief. He was not sure how she would react to his presence. "Hope you don't mind. I moved in with your parents." He paused. "I'll leave if you want me to."

"Of course you should stay!" she continued in her raspy voice. "Besides I gave you the name Mom to use, and I can't take it back." Looking towards Savannah, she whispered, "She's my Mama now!" After letting this sink in, Kara leaned over again to Jeremy. "You know you are going to have to take my room. I don't think I can walk up the stairs. You better pray first, though. It's pretty dark in there."

Savannah suddenly had a jolting thought. "Kara, we cleaned out your room! I am so sorry! We gave your paints away! I can buy more!" Fear taunted the child's mother. She was sure Kara would be angry.

Instead Kara smiled. "I don't want any more. I was done with the paints anyway. I don't want anything that was in that room except for my bible. And the paintings were so dark. Please throw them away. I don't want to remember them." She paused. "I can move my arms but my hands feel a bit clumsy. I doubt I will do anything that detailed again." Kara again hesitated. "Mama? I can barely feel my legs."

The three visitor's eyes were filled with tears. David's voice broke the silence. "If God can bring you back to us, he can heal your hands and legs."

"Yes, Daddy, He can. But I don't think He's going to, at least not all the way. I think He has other plans." Marveling at the change in this child, they remained silent. At least she seemed satisfied with her fate. The three remained puzzled that she had still not asked about the others that were in the car during the accident, but they quieted their hearts with the belief that she would ask when she was ready for the answer.

There was a lot of excitement outside the room as staff members observed the four talking. The tall slender young doctor entered, appearing momentarily at a loss for what to say. Examining Kara's extremities, he began speaking to her parents. "There has been a lot of damage. I think therapy is in order to see if she can get some of the movement back in her extremities. And we need to do some wound debridement, as some of the glass from the accident is still buried in Kara's skin." He hesitated. "Some of it will have to work its own way out, it is so deep. It will be quite painful."

"When can I go home?" Kara asked. "I want to leave the hospital."

The doctor hesitated. He had planned to keep her in the hospital throughout the treatments he proposed but secretly felt a bit of relief in the idea of getting some of the media attention away from the facility. This event was after all a bit of an embarrassment for him, as he had been the one insistent on turning off all life support systems, proclaiming that there was no hope. He decided that placing her into outpatient treatments might be more palatable for everyone. "As soon as you begin to eat normally," he answered, uneasily addressing the child he had pronounced dead just a short time ago. He was also unwilling to acknowledge a miracle as yet. Excusing himself, he slipped quietly from the room.

Everyone was convinced that Kara's eagerness to be discharged was a healthy sign of getting well. They were not privy to the discourse in her heart, as she listened to the plans of her Lord. They could not see her bleeding heart and the stripes embedded deep within her soul. Nor could they perceive the new name written on her forehead or know she had come back to them for but a little while. The day would quickly approach when all was complete, and she would lie once again in the arms of her Savior. The night approached when her wounded heart would answer His call, and her scarred frame would live no more.

....

Kara was glad to be out of the hospital, back in her parents' house. She was staying in the guest room down stairs to make it easier for Savannah to care for her. The press continued to hound the family, requesting interviews with Kara. To date, they had all been refused access. Kara could see the tiredness on Savannah's face. She knew it was difficult for her mother to continuously shield her from their constant attempts to talk with her, the girl who had come back from the dead. "Mama," she began, now her characteristic way of referring to her mother. "Mama, I'll talk with them if they promise to go away."

Savannah looked at her daughter hesitantly. She was concerned about how all the probing would affect her. She noticed Kara crying a lot at night when she thought no one was looking. She never talked about the accident or the nine months in the coma. Savannah was considering taking her daughter to a counselor to help her deal with what must be bothering her. Whenever she was taken for treatments, she insisted on refusing all pain medication, though the treatments were most assuredly excruciating. She just kept saying that she never wanted to be unaware of what they were doing to her, and no amount of coaxing changed her mind. It was clear that any attempt to override these desires would result in complete rejection of treatment. "Are you sure you are up to it?" She wondered if maybe, as painful as the memories must be, this would help her daughter to stop hiding her feelings, and she did so desperately want to get these people to leave them alone.

When David came home from work, husband and wife discussed Kara's suggestion and decided to take the risk. This was a chapter in their lives that needed closing, and this seemed to be the only way to do it. They felt that it might help all involved. They spoke with the press, insisting that there be one interview only, on the condition that they each sign an agreement to leave the family alone when it was done. They would be allowed one hour, in her room, the following day.

Kara barely ate that evening. Most foods caused intense pain going down her throat anyway. She was experiencing a great dread. She was afraid that they would try to make her into some type of heroine, and she knew the only true Hero was her King. She was afraid to be touched by the pride of men. Her scars and marks were acutely more painful than usual, a comfort to the child who desired nothing more than to remain unmarred by the stain of this darkness. She missed her Lord so terribly. At night she thought He visited her in her sleep, but in the daytime He seemed so very far away. It was as if the morning was her night, and her night was as the day. Jeremy spent quite a bit of his time waiting on her, and he sensed her intrepidation. Yet he remained silent on the issue, as he was learning that when she made decisions on matters of personal importance, there was no swaying her.

Kara entered into an uneasy sleep that night. She was playing over and over in her mind possible scenarios of the next day's interview. Yet when her body finally ceased its battle against slumber, she felt His kiss upon her cheek. He whispered something to her that she could not store in her mind, yet it brought her peace. His words returned to her written in Luke 12:11-12, "Now when they bring you to the synagogues and magistrates and authorities, do not worry about how or what you should answer, or what you should say. For the Holy Spirit will teach you in that very hour what you ought to say." (NKJV) Jeremy sat at her bedside all night, partly to give Savannah a break and partly out of curiosity. Her face seemed almost to glow at night, practically obscuring the scarring, and she was beautiful while she slept, though he dared share this with no one. Kara might not let him stay. He was sure she had experienced some encounter with the Savior during her coma, as the changes in her could be explained no other way. He was actually surprised that he was the only one who seemed to notice it.

Morning came too quickly for Kara. The rising sun seemed more like a veil of darkness to her than the greeting of a new day. Savannah gave her a bath and clothed her in her best outfit. "Mama," Kara started. "I am so sorry you have to work so hard to take care of me." Tears filled Savannah's eyes as she choked on the words she had to say.

"It's just so great to have you back, honey. I don't mind a bit." She took a breath and continued, "I am sorry I wasn't a better mother for you before the accident." The tears flowed freely down her cheeks.

"Oh no, Mama, that's not true!" She reached her feeble fingers to touch her mother's face. "That's not true at all! You did all you could do! I was just having a rough time like a lot of kids do. It wasn't your fault at all!" Savannah washed the tears from her daughter's face, unaware that every motion of her cloth on Kara's skin resulted in searing pain. Kara remained quiet, allowing her mother to finish her labor of love. "Mama?" she began again. "I dreamed about you a lot. I know about the things that happened to you. God showed me. You don't ever have to talk about it, though." She paused. "Mama? He saw the whole thing. He was there with you. It hurt Him, too, even more than it hurt you. Jesus showed me

226

your pain, but mostly He showed me His pain. He saw you raped and beaten, and He saw my sister killed. It hurt Him more than we can imagine. He saw you give Jeremy away, and He understood." Savannah was startled at first, in horror of what she was hearing. She was unable to restrain her tears. She would never have relayed her hurts so profoundly to anyone, though she was still at a loss, unclear as to how much Kara actually knew. "Mama, He needed to show me so I would understand. I am sorry I judged you." Savannah was unable to respond to her daughter's words, so she remained silent, simply kissing her daughter on the cheek. After tidying up the room, she washed her tears away. It was time for the press.

It seemed that a myriad of questions were slung at the child, completely overwhelming her. It was Jeremy who spoke first in her defense. "One question at a time, please," he insisted.

"Why are you back?" one reporter started. "Did God send you back, or do you think you were even dead at all?"

The room became silent, listening for the child's quiet voice. "God sent me back because, well, because He can. I think Mama and Daddy prayed too, and He loves them."

The barrage of questions resumed in full force. "What about the other five who died in the accident? Didn't their parents pray? Why did He leave you with all these scars? What did it feel like being dead?" Savannah was furious. How dare they mention the other children in the car! She was about to insist that they all leave, but Kara motioned to stop her, though the accusing words against her Lord stung as if she were being struck by whips again. She was feeling the pain of her Lord, with whom she had been so closely enmeshed.

"God deals with us individually. I don't know why they died. I only know God chooses what is best. And the scars, well," she was not about to fully explain. "Sometimes hard things and suffering helps us to get closer to Him." She fully ignored the question about what it feels like to be dead.

"So you are more important to God than the other five children?" one reporter quipped. It was as if another whip had landed with these barbed words.

"NO!" she fairly screamed. She began to cry. Her scars were stinging with a fury now, as if the lashes were landing on her once more. Before her family could insist that they all leave the room, however, Kara stopped them again.

Sensing that they were about to lose the interview, the voices of the reporters softened. "Is there one thing you want to tell us, something that would sum up your experience?" one gentler man asked.

Kara's reply came to rest in a part of every heart present, though many would choose not to admit it. "Jesus loves us all incredibly. He loves us with a passion. But He equally detests sin. He will do anything to get us to give it up. We never really get by with sin. He died so we wouldn't have to suffer the consequences of what we have done, but if we refuse what He offers, the consequences are worse than we can ever imagine. Even after He saves us, we have to let Him heal us from sin. It is a terrible disease.

But if we obey, being with Him is more wonderful than anything, and any amount of suffering is worth it, just to be with Him."

"For to me, to live is Christ, and to die is gain. But if I live on in the flesh, this will mean fruit from my labor; yet what I shall choose I cannot tell. For I am hard-pressed between the two, having a desire to depart and be with Christ, which is far better. Nevertheless to remain in the flesh is more needful for you." Philippians 1:21-24 (NKJV)

The reporters were stunned, but after a moment of regrouping, a full interrogation resulted. "So did you go to Heaven? Did you see Hell? Did you see God? What was He like?" The torrent of words were deafening to her ears. Kara refused to answer any more questions at this point, and the press was escorted from the room. Kara lay crying as they left. What she had experienced was too holy to be treated like this! She felt dirty, as if they had slung the most filthy black darkness at her with their words. Kara just cried, praying silently. She wanted so desperately to go Home. She wanted to be with Him. When David, Savannah, and Jeremy came back, she asked to be alone. But as they began to exit the room, she motioned for Jeremy to stay.

"Can you just read to me a bit?" she asked. "Can you read to me from my Bible?" He quickly agreed, grateful to be the one chosen for the task. She had confirmed his suspicions that she had been with the Master, and he wanted to spend any time with her that she would permit. Though he did not understand, she was allowing him to tip the bucket for her, as she was too feeble for the task. She was bathing in the water of His Word.

"Kara," he began softly, "you don't have to answer. But you were with Him, weren't you?" She nodded, tears filling her pillow. "He's the One you miss, isn't He? It's not Daniel at all." He paused as she said nothing. "Kara, I think He wants me to be a minister. I can't go to school right now. I am not even sure it would help anyway." At that she donned a faint smile through her tears. "But I am willing to learn from you whatever I can." Kara still said nothing, though she was beginning to trust the boy as a friend. "I love you, Kara. I am so glad you are my sister." At this he tried without success to stop his own tears. "Where do you want me to start reading?" he asked.

"Jeremy, tears are cleansing. Don't chase them away." He felt she was already teaching him. "You can start in Genesis and read as long as you can," she answered. She wanted so desperately for the whole bucket to be poured out, but she was so limited in this place. Her parched being was inexpressibly thirsty. In her heart, the bucket of His blood was overturned already, but she was at the mercy of another for this. Perhaps this too was a part of her Master's plan.

As he began to read, the words were a comfort to them both. Mostly the two said nothing, though occasionally Jeremy noticed an expression that caused him to wonder what she was thinking. At times she would interject a thought, which he cherished and placed in a holy closet in his being. He read about creation, and she remarked how sorrowful the Maker was at seeing it decaying before His eyes. Genesis 3:9-13 brought a special rise. "Then the LORD God called to Adam and said to him, 'Where are you?' So he said, 'I heard Your voice in the garden, and I was afraid because I was naked; and I hid myself.' And He said, 'Who told you that you were naked? Have you eaten from the tree of which I commanded you that you should not eat?' Then the man said, 'The woman whom You gave to be with me, she gave me of the tree, and I ate.' And the LORD God said to the woman, 'What is this you have done?' The woman said, 'The serpent deceived me, and I ate.'"(NKJV). Jeremy paused, seeing the intense suffering in her eyes. "Can I get you something, Kara? Are you alright?"

Kara ignored his questions but began instead to explain. "He hates it when we blame others like that. He wants us to take responsibility for our own sin. Adam was willing to let his wife die rather than face what he had done. I think that is why He tells men to be willing to give up their lives for their wives. Eve blamed the serpent. She should have listened to her husband, so now God tells wives to respect their husbands. It is all an answer to that first sin. Blaming others is the worst thing we can do when we get caught sinning." Jeremy read on until Kara fell asleep. But even in her sleep, a sadness seemed to come over her whenever he stopped. So Jeremy decided to remember at what place she fell asleep, as he did not want to miss any of her wisdom, but he read on and on. Jesus was planting His word in him as well. He read until she was awake again, and after her feeble attempt to eat her lunch, he began back at the point where she had fallen asleep. He became her own private attendant, not willing to leave her side. He left only when Savannah bathed her or helped her to the bathroom, sleeping in the chair beside her bed. Both David and Savannah marveled at the tenacity of the young man, not daring to come between the two, as Kara seemed to want him to stay. He had lost his job anyway, and it gave Savannah a break. As long as she brought meals to the two and cared for Kara's more private needs, the two were satisfied. Perhaps they were making up for lost time, Savannah thought.

Jeremy read unceasingly, stopping only to hear her comments. In Exodus he saw her pained expression as he continued: "Now when the people saw that Moses delayed coming down from the mountain, the people gathered together to Aaron, and said to him, 'Come, make us gods that shall go before us; for as for this Moses, the man who brought us up out of the land of Egypt, we do not know what has become of him.' And Aaron said to them, 'Break off the golden earrings which are in the ears of your wives, your sons, and your daughters, and bring them to me.' So all the people broke off the golden earrings which were in their ears, and brought them to Aaron. And he received the gold from their hand, and he fashioned it with an engraving tool, and made a molded calf. Then they said, 'This is your god, O Israel, that brought you out of the land of Egypt!'" Exodus 32:1-4 (NKJV) Her tears were flowing as a torrent at these words, and Jeremy desired deeply to understand.

"We make so many idols! They become gods to us, and He has to take them away! Then we get angry because He takes them, and He has to bring us to a place that we give them to Him willingly!" It seemed the lashes were as fresh as if they had been planted yesterday.

Jeremy paused. He was amazed even at his own thoughts. "Was it your art, Kara?" he whispered. He had seen the dark paintings before Kara insisted that they be destroyed. "Was that your god?" At this point the sobs were uncontrollable. "Do you miss it much?"

"No, I don't miss it at all. It was wretched after I polluted it. We ruin such wonderful things when we keep them from Him!" This shook the young man to the core. He knew this was a warning he must always heed. Though he could not comprehend her intensity, he dare not shrug it off. This was a holy lesson, a part of her very heart. He continued to read on. Kara cried as he read of Israel's punishment for their sin. Though Moses interceded, they still suffered a great consequence for their transgression. She wept as he related how Moses could only see a portion of God's glory, as Jesus had not yet come, knowing that God and sin could not coexist. Kara was saddened as they devoured the scripture, experiencing Moses' loss as he could not enter the promised land due to his own sin. She marveled as he faced his consequences while continuing to serve the people. Kara loved the institution of the Passover, as it portrayed the coming sacrifice of her King. Jeremy was amazed at her insatiable appetite for God's word, as it instilled the same longing in him as well. He knew that whenever this time was complete, he would never be the same. And though he did not want to admit it, even to himself, he knew their comradeship was only for a short time.

Kara could not put into words the meanings of the different rituals of the Law, though she recognized that they fit into the holiness she had experienced in a special way. The descriptions of the temple made her homesick beyond measure. Lamentations brought intense suffering, as she marveled at the consequences of refusing to repent, of turning to other gods, and remaining hardened still.

"How lonely sits the city
That was full of people!
How like a widow is she,
Who was great among the nations!
The princess among the provinces
Has become a slave!

She weeps bitterly in the night,
Her tears are on her cheeks;
Among all her lovers
She has none to comfort her.
All her friends have dealt treacherously with her;
They have become her enemies.

Judah has gone into captivity,

Under affliction and hard servitude;

She dwells among the nations,

She finds no rest;

All her persecutors overtake her in dire straits."

Lamentations 1:1-3 (NKJV)

Ezra and Nehemiah rebuilding the temple reminded her of how her Lord explained His sorrow over the state of His church, broken down and needing repairs. There were so many secrets hidden in His word, so much of the very nature of her Lord, and Jeremy wanted to hear it all. Kara was happy to have a true friend in this lonely place, though there were things she could not share even with him. They had grown so very close, as he read to her day after day, excited to hear any bit of wisdom from her.

The New Testament brought more revelations, with the crucifixion being especially painful, as she remembered how her lashes landed so fully on Him. Reading of Peter's failure in denying his Lord reminded the pair of their own failures. The resurrection gave them hope, and the teachings of Paul brought perspective on living for Christ in this earth. They read 1 Corinthians 4:5, "Therefore judge nothing before the time, until the Lord comes, who will both bring to light the hidden things of darkness and reveal the counsels of the hearts. Then each one's praise will come from God." (NKJV) They were reminded of how insufficient man's judgment is, not knowing the end of a thing. Kara became especially quiet as he read 2 Corinthians 5:1-4, "For we know that if our earthly house, this tent, is destroyed, we have a building from God, a house not made with hands, eternal in the heavens. For in this we groan, earnestly desiring to be clothed with our habitation which is from heaven, if indeed, having been clothed, we shall not be found naked. For we who are in this tent groan, being burdened, not because we want to be unclothed, but further clothed, that mortality may be swallowed up by life." (NKJV)

1 John 3:1-3 captivated them, as they read of His love for them, "Behold what manner of love the Father has bestowed on us, that we should be called children of God! Therefore the world does not know us, because it did not know Him. Beloved, now we are children of God; and it has not yet been revealed what we shall be, but we know that when He is revealed, we shall be like Him, for we shall see Him as He is. And everyone who has this hope in Him purifies himself, just as He is pure." Kara shared a bit with Jeremy of her Lord's hatred for sin and how He desires it be dealt with here, in the body, faced willingly and repented of.

Revelations was especially comforting to Kara, as it made her feel more in His presence. Day after day, the word was poured out in this place. Kara's heart was growing sadder, as she missed the King greatly. She ached to be in His presence, to walk openly with Him again.

Jeremy asked her many questions, gleaning all he could. Kara laughed inwardly, as he seemed glued to her side as Elisha was to Elijah, afraid of missing something. She teased him a bit about it, though she knew that she was nothing great; but Jeremy knew she had been with Him and was not willing to let go without a battle. Question after question, he tried to learn. "What do you think of communion?" he asked. "What does it mean?" This started a major discourse, as she had thought on it a lot.

"Well," she began, "Jesus started that at the last supper. He was sharing a Passover meal with them before He had to suffer on the cross. It was one of their last times together before His death and resurrection. He told them to share it together in remembrance of Him later. He said that the bread stood for His body and the cup for His blood. Jesus is called the Word, our daily bread, and His blood was given for our salvation. His body was broken on the cross, just like at the meal, and sometimes because of us, His body seems to be broken still, as the church is divided into groups that fight with each other. It was at that supper that Judas betrayed Him. I think it is a very important picture He has given to us." Jeremy waited, sure she knew more. "It seems like everyone concentrates on the part in 1 Corinthians 11:27-31: 'Therefore whoever eats this bread or drinks this cup of the Lord in an unworthy manner will be guilty of the body and blood of the Lord. But let a man examine himself, and so let him eat of the bread and drink of the cup. For he who eats and drinks in an unworthy manner eats and drinks judgment to himself, not discerning the Lord's body. For this reason many are weak and sick among you, and many sleep. For if we would judge ourselves, we would not be judged.' (NKJV) They concentrate on their own sins instead of on what Jesus did on the cross. He said we were to do this in remembrance of Him. I think Paul was talking about getting our attitudes right instead of scarfing down a meal without thinking about what it meant. Also, since the Body of Christ is the Church, I think He was referring to how we view one another. His Body, which was broken, scattered, even marred with sin for our sakes, is more than the physical flesh He embodied here on earth. We are the Body of Christ, individually scattered as the bread, individually sacred in His sight. He wants us to respect each other for how valuable each one is to Him, not thinking we are any more important than anyone else. The Corinthians he was scolding were coming in selfishness, seeing who could eat first or get the most. Their thoughts were for filling their stomachs rather than keeping the memory of Christ's death and resurrection. They lost sight of the very thing Jesus desired … the respect for His body. We still have to deal with our sin, but at that table, we should be thinking of Him. If we have bad attitudes towards others, we should take care of it before we even come."

"I don't think it matters how often people choose to observe it or what type of symbols they use. Some use a sweet bread, some a dry cracker, and some serve wine while others serve gape juice. If anything, this just makes it clear how varied His body is. We should be able to do this practice with all types of groups and in different ways, as long as it is done in remembrance of Him, signifying His death and resurrection on our behalf."

"Another thing I think is important," she continued, "is that we respect what happens when we come into God's presence, which is a part of what happens at communion but applies to other times as well. People in churches ask God for His presence, but they really don't understand what they are requesting. When we truly come into His presence, we are faced with a powerful choice. He will reveal our sin just by being there, because He is perfect. That is unavoidable, as He is holy. We must either repent so that He can take our sin away, or something very serious happens. We can become more solid in our sinfulness. There is a certain sealing, or permanence, that takes place, whatever choice we make. That is the secret of Revelations 22:11: 'He that is unjust, let him be unjust still: and he which is filthy, let him be filthy still: and he that is righteous, let him be righteous still: and he that is holy, let him be holy still.' (NKLV). Sometimes He holds back His presence to give people more time to consider their decision, to keep a bad choice from being finalized. We really don't understand the holiness of God."

"What do you think water baptism is about?" he asked. "I mean, it seems to be just a ritual."

Kara smiled that smile that made Jeremy sure she was hearing from her Lord. "Well, we are taught in the Bible that we are buried in baptism, symbolic of our old life being buried with Jesus' death. Water is also symbolic of His word that brings death and judgment to sin but brings life to those that believe. Coming out of the water, we take part in His resurrection and are born again into His new life, arising from our grave. I think God uses symbols, as a testimony and proclamation of what He has done in our lives. Just as many of the prophets like Elijah did a lot of strange things in order to paint a picture of what God was saying, He causes us to show things by our actions as well. We are proclaiming through baptism that we accept what Jesus has done for us on the cross and that we are willing to die to our old way of life in order to have His new life instead. In a way, we are announcing to the world that we will take up our cross and follow Him. In this, we accept both His suffering and His joy. We are stating that we belong to Christ and that He belongs to us. It is an outward sign that our relationship with Him is sealed forever in our hearts." Kara smiled. "You know, maybe in a way I am a living picture. I was in a coma for nine months, in a grave of sleep, before I came back. It is just like it takes nine months to have a baby. It was like a new birth, I suppose. It was also like coming out of a tomb in a way, only it feels kind of backwards to me. It was better there with Him. That world is actually much more real than this, as it is not a place where sin deceives as it does here. Of course the sin in your heart needs to be purged away before you go all the way in. If you don't listen to Him here, that can be a very difficult process."

Jeremy looked at her again, noting the sadness in her eyes. He knew she was longing for the King. He wished he knew what she had seen. He decided to pose another question. "Do you think God cares about our governments? I mean, do elections even matter for Christians? I haven't decided if I will vote in the coming election or not. It is so much a part of the world anyway."

Kara thought for a moment. "Well," she began. "I am sure it matters, because in the Bible God says 'By Me kings reign, And rulers decree justice.' Proverbs 8:15(NKJV). Since He arranges

these things, I am sure that He cares. He says also 'Woe t
land, when your king is a child, and your princes feast in the
morning!' Ecclesiastes 10:16(NKJV). So who the ruler is does affec
a nation. Over and over, Israel went through terrible sorrows because
of evil kings, and He took great care in choosing their rulers. Even
King David's sins affected the people, though he was a good king."

"But in our country, the president has very limited power.
Should we just be concerned about congress?" he prodded.

"Well, I think that there is actually a lot more than that going
on, especially in a country that chooses its own leaders. If we choose
men that are ungodly, it is a reflection of our evil hearts. I think we
are making a statement before God, and if the wickedness of our
chosen leader is great enough, we may be inviting God's judgment
on our land. Each person, I suppose, must follow his own conscience
in the matter, whether by prayer or voting or however God speaks to
him. But no matter what, I think it is important, since we are told to
pray for those in governmental authority. If you follow through the
scriptures, as we have together, over and over a line of authority is
set forth. Even though men have abused it, there is no denying that it
is there. Jesus chose the apostles, as well as many other leaders, to
show us the way to God. I think by the natural order of things, it is
obvious that He is very selective in the process. It seems like
practically everything works that way. Even in Heaven, there are
elders around the throne, and even Lucifer was assigned over many
angels before he fell."

"That brings up another question," piped up Jeremy. "What was all that about, creating Lucifer even though he would fall? Surely God knew that would happen. Sometimes it doesn't seem to make sense. Wouldn't it have been easier not to create him at all?"

Kara smiled. "I really don't think God is that interested in making things easier. I think He would rather make them right. He is all about free will and choice. There had to be a choice, even in Heaven, for good to appear completely good. He doesn't make robots, and He makes no mistakes. He would rather have friends. Evil had to be a choice, though He would prefer no one chose that way. Lucifer was created beautiful and perfect. He had the life of God in him to create, before he squandered it away. Evil came from his own choice, and what a powerful entity it became! Yet as Satan he cannot give life, as there is only death and destruction in him. The angels under him followed his bad example, thus the demonic realm was formed. When Adam and Eve sinned in the garden, they introduced that blackness into God's perfect Earth. They polluted the whole land. That is one reason they had to leave the garden, besides the fact that if they stayed and ate of the tree of life, they would have been under Satan's thumb forever, just like the creatures that already followed him. The sentence of death, formerly belonging to Satan and the fallen angels, came upon them. Death had to destroy their corrupt bodies to completely demolish the sin in them. It took their bodies a long time to completely die, as God had created them perfectly. But the death within them eventually accomplished the job, as it was so very evil. That is why it is such a great victory in

Christ when death is defeated forever. 'For this corruptible mus[t]
on incorruption, and this mortal must put on immortality. So when
this corruptible has put on incorruption, and this mortal has put on
immortality, then shall be brought to pass the saying that is written:
"Death is swallowed up in victory. "O Death, where is your sting? O
Hades, where is your victory?" The sting of death is sin, and the
strength of sin is the law. But thanks be to God, who gives us the
victory through our Lord Jesus Christ. Therefore, my beloved
brethren, be steadfast, immovable, always abounding in the work of
the Lord, knowing that your labor is not in vain in the Lord.' 1
Corinthians 15:53-58 (NKJV) If you notice, God does not restore
our earthly bodies when we get to Heaven. He gives us a new one.
Our bodies are the part that dies, and God redeems our souls that our
souls and spirits would always be with Him. People don't
understand that sin has to be dealt with, permanently destroyed in us.
God does not want another rebellion in Heaven, so it is necessary
that the darkness be demolished in us. This is a painful process, as
we allow Him to transform us into His image. It means we truly
have to turn our backs on sin. If we do not do this willingly, the
process can become an agonizing event. It is very important to Him
to keep the balance between free will and the absolute absence of
sin."

"What do you think about people complaining about what
they see as contradictions in the Bible?" Jeremy asked. "How do you
answer that for them?"

"An apparent contradiction means something is missing in our understanding. The different gospels, for instance, include different facts. It is like two people looking at the same thing from different angles. They both relate a part of the picture, and if you put the two together, you see more of the whole thing. Both are correct, but they look different if you look at them separately. God is not wrong, but our understanding gets confused in this evil world. If we seriously want to know the truth of a thing, all we have to do is to ask Him. We still may not understand completely right away, but it will come. He will tell us what we really need to know, but it is our job to trust Him, not just to challenge His authority constantly. It comes with relationship with Him," she replied emphatically.

The boy leaned back in his chair to absorb these things. He was sure she possessed a wisdom well beyond her age, a wisdom that could only come from being with the Master. His love for His Lord expanded so much just being around her. Then he began to ask her another question. "Some people say God has called this generation to bring about His changes, that this is a very special time to follow Him. What do you think about that?"

Kara thought for a moment, her brother thinking it seemed like she was listening to something. "Well," she began, "God has been calling generation after generation to follow Him completely. Sometimes we respond to the call for a little while before we give up. He is definitely calling again. He is asking that we respond without making excuses. God doesn't like excuses at all. He considers them dishonest and selfish. Even though parents or friends

244

have not done these things, we are each to take a stand. Just like the children of Israel disobeyed and were stuck in the desert for forty years, some of the people that went before us were stuck too. If we use them as an excuse not to obey, we will share their fate. I bet those parents warned their children not to make the same mistakes they made. At least they must have listened, because Joshua was able to lead them into the promised land. Then they saw their own miracle, as the Jordan river was dried up before them, and it was time for their own relationship with God based on more than what their parents had told them."

"I think today is much like that. There are still some people like Joshua and Caleb who follow God and will help lead the way. But God doesn't want us to wait for others to do what He has put in our hearts to accomplish. It is time to follow before any more are lost. We complain that there are people who have never heard about God, like it's His fault. It's really our fault for refusing to obey. That's what you have to do, Jeremy. You have to let God use you to help others, whether anyone recognizes what you do or not."

"Why do you think people hate each other so much? I mean, they judge each other by race and other things over which no one has any control anyway. It doesn't make any sense," the boy mused.

"I think people are scared of anything different from them. Sin brings fear, and fear leads to all kinds of foolish decisions. Satan wants to use those differences against us, as he always likes to twist what God made. Those very differences were created to enrich our lives, to cause us to learn from one another. If we hate in this way, not only do we damage our own conscience, but we miss out on wonderful relationships as well. We all have so much to teach each other, so many rich experiences to share. We all can share from our own cultures what Jesus has planted in us. This hatred is so far from what God wants for us, as He has asked us to love one another, actually considering others as more important than ourselves." Kara lay back and rested. With Jeremy's help, the bucket had been poured out.

Chapter 10

Savannah worked in the kitchen preparing lunch for Jeremy and Kara. She was amazed by how these two had become inseparable. It seemed they were intent on doing nothing but reading the Bible and talking. Though she was happy to see this, she was somewhat concerned about Kara's state of mind. She often caught Kara crying at night when she thought no one noticed, and occasionally she would cry out in her sleep, as if calling someone to her. Savannah was convinced she was still mourning for Daniel, who had been killed in the accident. When she discussed this with David, the idea of counseling came up. Were these recent actions, burying herself in her Bible and speaking almost exclusively to Jeremy, an expression of her guilt for being the only one left alive? The reporters had so abruptly informed her of the fates of the other children in the accident. Savannah did not even bother telling Kara what the reporters wrote. Some of them twisted her words terribly, though a couple presented an unadulterated version.

The phone rang. When Savannah answered, the girl on the other end asked to speak to Kara. "Who is this?" asked Savannah, hoping it was not another reporter. The voice on the other end just claimed to be a friend of Kara's. Taking the phone with her, Savannah entered Kara's room. "Kara, a girl named Jackie wants to talk with you." Kara caught her breath, and at first Savannah thought she would refuse the call. However Kara reached out her feeble arm for the phone instead.

"Can I talk to Jackie alone?" she asked. Savannah and Jeremy left the room. "Hi, Jackie," she began.

"Hey, you're still alive! Guess God didn't want you after all. He threw you back!" she laughed. The words landed like barbs.

"Jackie, I have to tell you something," Kara started.

"Oh great," Jackie replied. "I read about you in the papers. Are you going to get all religious on me?"

"Jackie, God loves you. And He didn't make you gay, any more than He made me do the sins I did. We all have to face our sins, no matter how big or small that sin appears to us. He wants to change your life. Just because you are tempted to sin doesn't mean God made you that way. He can help you out of your sin just like He helps people out of other sins, but you have to let Him do it."

"Yeah, right!" Jackie retorted, making sure to add a few profanities, and she abruptly hung up the phone. Kara cried and cried. She ached for her friend, wishing she could change what had been. At least she had gotten to try. When Savannah came back, the child could not be comforted. She became angry that someone had affected her child like this, and Kara gave no answers to her prying. Savannah determined that counseling was definitely in order. She called and made an appointment right away.

By the time Jeremy returned, Kara was calmer. He hurt for his sister, not knowing what had transpired on the phone, much less how it was connected to the nine months she had spent in a coma. Everything seemed to be connected to the time she spent with her Lord. Jeremy sometimes wished he could tell Savannah more about his conversations with Kara, but he knew that his sister had taken him into her confidence, and he must not betray it. "Kara," he started gently, "do you want to read more today? We can start all over if you want."

Kara smiled and asked him to read from the Psalms, which brought her comfort. But before he could begin, she made another request of him. "When I die, will you speak at my funeral?" The boy was stunned. "And give people an opportunity to accept Jesus? Will you tell them I loved Jesus more than anything and that I have been missing Him so?"

"Kara, they say you get stronger every day. But if I am still alive, of course I will do that for you. But let's not talk like that right now." She smiled, satisfied with his response, and the reading began. "The Lord is my shepherd; I shall not want. He makes me to lie down in green pastures; He leads me beside the still waters. He restores my soul; He leads me in the paths of righteousness For His name's sake. Yea, though I walk through the valley of the shadow of death, I will fear no evil; For You are with me; Your rod and Your staff, they comfort me. You prepare a table before me in the presence of my enemies; You anoint my head with oil; My cup runs over. Surely goodness and mercy shall follow me All the days of my life; And I will dwell in the house of the Lord Forever." Psalms 23:1-6 (NKJV) Kara smiled, thinking about her Lord. Even here, He did lead her. Even here, He did restore her. Even in this place, she was kept safe by His rod of correction, by His staff that kept her from going astray. He provided for her in the presence of her enemies, and he had given her rest. He had given her more than enough. Tears flowed down her face, however, as she missed Him so much.

Their reading was interrupted by Savannah's entrance into the room. "We need to take you for your skin treatment," she started. Hesitantly she continued. "Kara, we want you to talk with a counselor while we are out." Kara did not reply. Though the treatments were softening the severity of her scars, she knew her Lord could see what was inside. As for the therapist, she figured God knew how to give her the words to get through the situation. Perhaps this was an appointment made by Him anyway. Jeremy left the room so Savannah could get Kara ready, and afterwards he returned to help Savannah get her out of bed. Kara had regained enough function to stand a little with help, using her weak arms to move towards the wheelchair. David was waiting at the van to assist as well, and after getting everyone situated, they were off.

David thought Kara seemed exceptionally quiet on the ride, perhaps a bit sullen. He wondered if she was upset at the notion of seeing a counselor. It was difficult for him to read her at all anymore. Though her attitude had improved beyond imagination since the accident, he felt he didn't even know her any longer. She seemed aged well beyond her years, as if she was older and wiser than any of them. Yet she was a child, ready to turn sixteen in a few days.

Kara's treatments caused her to sustain the usual searing pain, as wounds were cleaned, small pieces of glass eliminated, old skin removed, and all was redressed. No one even bothered to attempt to convince her to take pain medicine anymore, as she had always refused. She smiled as she left, disarming them completely. "Jesus loves you," she proclaimed. "He really does you know. He wants your friendship, too." The staff frequently seemed unable to resist her charm, and workers allowed her to pray with them, many accepting Jesus as their Lord on more than one occasion. It was amazing to them that she could love Him so much in the face of her sufferings, and they were sure she knew something that they did not.

The visit with the therapist was to follow. Kara was taken into a room, softly lit and comfortably furnished. A pleasant perfumed aroma was in the air, in this room of pale blue walls and light brown furnishings. As the counselor entered, Kara could not help but think there was a sadness in her eyes. She was about five foot seven inches tall, straight blond hair about shoulder length, well dressed in a woman's blue business suit. "My name is Sandy," she started, reaching out to shake her hand. "And you are Kara?" Kara nodded, waiting for what would come next. She had never talked to a therapist before. After wheeling the child into her office space, the woman began speaking with Kara. "Tell me a little about yourself," the thin woman of about thirty began.

Unsure of what to say, Kara hesitated. "I am nearly sixteen. I am not in school right now because I have been recovering from a bad accident. I am sure you heard about it."

The therapist nodded. "Why have you decided to wait to restart your schooling? There are agencies that would send someone to your home." Kara did not respond. "Do you think it's because you are depressed?" When she still could get no rise from Kara, she determined to try probing a bit deeper. "Your mother says that she keeps hearing you crying in your sleep saying you miss someone. Do you miss the boy you were with on the night of the accident?" She thought she hit a nerve when Kara's eyes opened wide, so she waited for a response. "Is that it, Kara? Do you feel guilty because you are here and he is not?"

Tears were flowing down Kara's cheeks, convincing the therapist she was definitely making progress. "No," Kara whispered with a puzzled look on her face. "That's not it at all!" She hesitated. "I don't even want to be here! There is so much more than this!"

Still believing she had created a successful interview, the therapist asked, "Do you think you would ever hurt yourself?"

"Oh no!" Kara replied. "He would never be happy with that!"

"Who, Kara? Who would be unhappy? Daniel?"

Kara looked up at her in amazement. This woman had absolutely no idea what she was talking about. "Not Daniel. I am sorry he died, but I don't miss Daniel! I miss Jesus! I just want to be with Him!"

It looked as if she had slapped the therapist across the face. Kara could not know that the woman had turned away from a relationship with her Lord several years prior, and this time it was Kara who hit a nerve. She had no idea that the woman had entered this profession to hide from her own problems or that she had just brought a multitude of suppressed hurts to the surface. Kara was simply being Kara, simply replying to the woman as she knew how. The therapist abruptly ended the interview and rolled her chair out the door. Addressing Savannah, the therapist said, "You need to get another practitioner. She has problems that I cannot help her with. There will be no charge for today."

As they lifted Kara into the car, everyone was silent. Jeremy leaned over to Kara and whispered in her ear. "You told her, didn't you." Kara nodded, tears flowing down her face. She felt so sorry for the therapist, as she had caught a glimpse into the woman's soul. The weight of resentment was great, devouring the woman's very being and tainting her entire view on life. It was like a fungus, creeping deep into her being.

David started the conversation first. "How are you feeling?" he asked Kara. "Are you too tired for a visit to Grandma's? She really wants to see you." Kara hesitated. Grandma hadn't visited since the accident. How could she even relate to her? Still she felt this visit was probably ordained of God, so she consented. They drove through a local burger joint for food, but she only ordered a milkshake. She did not want to try to force solid foods past the strictures in her throat, especially in the car.

The drive to Grandma's was without incident, as Kara stared out the window at the greenery about them. The trees were all green, with a few colored leaves, an early sign of fall a few months away. The ride seemed momentary, though it look about thirty minutes, as Kara was enthralled by the beauty of her Lord's creation. Those lovely, colorful flowers still decorated the neighborhood, though Kara was sure it was nothing to compare with the beauty she had seen. The vividness of the sights her Lord had shown her seemed to be fading in her mind in this dark place, adding to her sadness. This place that had offered so much peace before seemed quite hollow to her now. Only Dad still had his refuge here. The roses were in full bloom, lining the drive to this red brick home, and the lawn was still shaded by the large green tree. Grandma came to the car to meet them, escorting them into her home. Cheery as usual, Grandma hugged her son and kissed Kara on the cheek. "It's been a long time," she told Kara. "I've missed you. Seems you've become quite a celebrity! Everyone wants to know about the little girl that came back from the dead." Grandma couldn't possibly know that her comment would sting, as it smacked too much of the pride of men for Kara's appetite.

Kara turned towards Jeremy, who was merely standing beside her, feeling a bit awkward. "This is my brother, Grandma. This is Jeremy. He is also a great friend." As Grandma politely shook his hand, Kara began again. Turning to Savannah, she said, "and this is my Mama!" Grandma was shook to the core. She knew exactly what Kara meant. This was her way of telling her grandmother that she was not willing to hear anything bad about her mother, and that if Grandma did not accept Savannah, it would be a personal affront to the child.

David sat in the same big arm chair, and he ushered Savannah and Jeremy to the old couch with the orange and white

254

afghan. Kara was parked beside the window in a wheel chair. Grandma puttered in the kitchen, recovering from the shock of what had just taken place. She had prepared a desert for the visit, and the aroma of the cherry cobbler filled the room. Savannah offered to help, and Grandma seemed unable to resist the quip. "Sure, my maid is off for the day," she replied. "You can clean the bathroom while you are at it." David nearly jumped from his seat as he headed for the kitchen.

"Mom, Savannah is not a maid! She is my wife and the mother of my child!" Grandma started to cry. David had never talked to her that way before, but she knew he was right. She hugged Savannah and apologized.

"We both know that I have never accepted you," she whispered. "I am so sorry. You have been the best daughter-in-law possible, and I have never given you a chance. I can make all the excuses I want, but I know it was wrong. My husband tried for years before he died to tell me. Please forgive me, Savannah." Savannah's heart melted. Nodding between her tears, she was completely overcome with the healing within her. Savannah now had a mom.

The cherry cobbler was especially tasty, covered with vanilla ice cream. There was so much joy and peace in the place. They barely noticed that Kara was not eating with them. She spent the time looking satisfied as she glanced upon each face. She caught a glimpse of what Jesus was saying to His disciples when He told them that His food was to do His Father's will. Dad had finally stood up for Savannah, Mama had a mom, and Jeremy had a family.

Even Jeremy was being included in the conversation, which was light and happy, and all present seemed to be enveloped in the peace of her King. What better desert could there be than that?

The ride home was exceptionally pleasant, as all reveled in the healings of the hour. They seemed to have forgotten the therapist's remarks, which was a relief to Kara. She was sure this trip had been orchestrated by Someone far greater than anyone in this place.

....

Kara's birthday was fast approaching, and Savannah and Jeremy busied themselves with preparations. She wouldn't tell them what she wanted but just put them off, informing them that she did not desire any gifts for her birthday. Kara didn't dare inform them of what she wanted most, anyway. They insisted, however, so Kara settled on a tape player/recorder. She said she would like some music tapes to play and some empty tapes on which to record. She secretly knew Mama had an old player she could give her, as money was tight with all the medical bills. They would only need to buy the tapes. The request seemed to satisfy everyone, and they busied themselves getting it cleaned up and wrapped for her. Her true desires could only be met by her Lord anyway. Kara was too homesick to notice all the activity. She missed the King so much.

Jeremy entered the room and asked if he could read to her. She quickly agreed. She listened as he read from Philippians, and she cried when she heard verses twenty-three and twenty-four of chapter one: "For I am hard-pressed between the two, having a desire to depart and be with Christ, which is far better. Nevertheless to remain in the flesh is more needful for you." (NKJV)

"Jeremy?" she interrupted. As he looked up from his task, she continued. "Will you take care of Mama when I am gone?"

Jeremy felt like his heart was breaking, as if someone had shoved a knife into his chest. Why did she insist on talking about dying? The thought put a lump in his throat. He could see that this was important to her, however, so he promised. Then she handed him a scribbled piece of paper on which she had managed to write a poem. "Here. You will know what to do with this at the right time." Opening the paper, he read it and stored it between the covers of his Bible. It read:

THREE CROSSES

Three crosses
In my soul;
I can see the crucifixion
Of me …..

Two thieves were crucified
With my Savior;
One thief died,
One thief was reborn
And My Savior rose again.

Three crosses,

Three tombs sealed;

One thief is ever dying

One thief is reborn

And my Savior

Is ever alive within.

Jeremy continued to read, his heart still aching. He, more than anyone else, knew that she was homesick, but he was afraid of losing her. He left the room sadly after she fell asleep, as she seemed to be at peace.

Alone in his room, Jeremy contemplated his fears. He had depended on Kara so much these past two months. She seemed to be getting better physically, but he could not shake her words. He could hear his Lord speaking in his heart, so he began listening intently. "Who is your teacher, Jeremy?" Though he had gleaned a great deal from Kara, He knew what God was getting at. The Holy Spirit was his real Teacher. Yet his heart still cried that he would miss her so. He had only had a sister to spend time with for two months, and they had grown painfully close. He would rather experience nearly any loss than that of the friendship of his sister. "Can you let her go, Jeremy? What if I am ready to take her home?" Jeremy began to cry. He knew any answer besides yes was not only wrong but unfair to Kara as well. His wounded heart acquiesced, and as he began to drift off to sleep, he heard something that troubled his soul. "Will you forgive him, Jeremy? Will you forgive?" Though he had no idea what the words meant, they lodged deep within his soul.

In the next room, David was fighting his own battle. Savannah was in the kitchen, and God's voice in his heart was strong again. David knew that whenever he heard God this clearly, it was something very important. "What do you think about My daughter?" his Lord began. The words stung, as David was keenly aware of what He was getting at. He was being reminded that Kara was not his own. "She is amazing, don't you think?" his Lord went on. "See what great things I have done in your family through her?"

"Yes, Lord," David responded, a dryness in his throat.

"She is merely on loan to you, David. If you love her, you will understand." Tears were streaming down the man's face as he acknowledged what His Maker was telling him. "She's yours, Lord. I understand. One day you may take her, and I have to love you just the same." He sensed his King smiling on him, as He comforted his heart. He too fell asleep with a question ringing in his ears, an inquisition that completely puzzled him. "Will you forgive him, David? Will you forgive?"

Savannah had just finished cleaning in the kitchen when she sat down for a rest. She felt the yearning in her being that was always there when her Father called her to Himself. She turned off the light and went into the living room, climbing into the big brown chair, and she visualized herself in her Father's lap. He smiled at her, a smile she could sense but not see. "Thank you for coming, for listening to My Voice." She heard Him so clearly. "It is time for you to sit with Me and be My friend." She snuggled up a while, expressing her love for the King, and she felt His sorrow as He began to speak again. "Do you really love Me, Savannah?" He asked, cutting her to the quick.

"Of course!" she replied. "Thank you so much for all you have done for me and for our family!"

"But do you love Me, even if you can't keep them all? Do you love Me more than these?" Savannah was horrified. "Please, Lord, don't take them! Please let them stay!"

"But what if I need them? Will you still love Me?"

Savannah began to cry. She knew what the only right answer was, but it was so hard. Finally she squeezed the words through her lips, as though she were wringing out her very heart like a rag. "Yes, Lord. I will always love You, and I trust Your judgment." He held her close as she continued to cry, until she finally fell asleep, barely hearing the question that troubled her mind. "Will you forgive him, Savannah? Will you forgive?" It would be a big day tomorrow, as it was Kara's sixteenth birthday.

....

The whole house was in an uproar as everyone prepared for Kara's birthday. No one talked about their encounters from the night before, each believing it to be his own private experience. Savannah was getting Kara dressed, and Jeremy was icing the cake. Amidst the commotion, the phone rang. Dad brought it to Kara. Savannah nearly stopped him, afraid of what this conversation would bring, but Kara insisted on answering the phone. They all stepped out at her request. "Hello?" Kara began.

"This is Jackie," the voice began, as Kara braced herself. "Listen, Kara, I am really sorry about the last time I called. I've been thinking about what you said." Kara waited, relieved at the words on the other end. "Well I am not sure about everything yet, but I just wanted to let you know that I will be considering what you said."

"I love you, Jackie," Kara answered. "Do you want me to pray with you?"

"No," Jackie replied. "Not yet anyway. Just wanted to let you know."

"Do you want to come over? My family is having a party for me. It's my birthday."

"No, I really can't, but happy birthday. And thanks. You can pray for me by yourself if you want."

"I will," Kara replied. "I do a lot, Jackie."

"Well, goodbye," Jackie responded and hung up. Kara did pray for Jackie again, and she thanked her Lord for the birthday present, the call from Jackie. Almost immediately, the phone rang again. This time it was Kara's old friend, Susanna, on the line. They hadn't talked since the accident.

"Wow, I haven't talked to you in so long!" Susanna started. "I have been hearing so much about you and reading about you in the papers. I didn't even get to tell you about our trip to Kentucky. It was so much fun!" Kara had almost forgotten how to make small talk, so she was silent. "Are you still there?" she continued.

"Yes," answered Kara. "How have you been?"

"Ok, I guess. Oh, happy birthday! Well, I am kind of mad at my mom today. She just bought my sister a new outfit, and she didn't even get one for me. It's not fair!" She paused, then started again. "Don't you think she should get me stuff, too? Sandy always gets more than me!"

"Well," Kara started, the words echoing hollowly in her ears, "God doesn't always make things exactly even either, and He is the perfect parent. He just knows what is best for each of us. Jesus told a story about some workers, each starting at a different time of the day. When they got paid, the boss gave everyone the same amount of money, though some only worked part of the day. When they complained that it wasn't fair, he basically told them that he had the right to give extra to the others as well. I think he was teaching us not to compare ourselves with others, since we don't understand the whole picture. Maybe your mom knew that your sister needed the clothes and couldn't afford to buy extras for you. Or maybe she knew your sister was having a bad day. Anyway, I think we are supposed to be grateful for what we have and not compare it with what others get."

"They were right," she grumbled. "Everyone told me you were like this. What happened to you? You are actually defending my mother against me!"

"God has just been teaching me a lot, that's all. I am beginning to understand that even what we consider small sins are ugly to Him. He wants to help us get rid of the sin."

"So I am sinning because I am mad at my mom? You really have changed. I am not sure I like it," Susanna replied.

"I can't change who I am, Susanna. My life is completely given to God. He does look at the attitudes of our hearts, and He wants to change anything that is not right in us. Sooner or later, we all face Him. Sooner or later, we have to answer for our sins."

"Well, happy birthday. I really don't want to talk about this anymore, so I think I'll go," stated Susanna.

"I love you, Susanna, and so does Jesus." Kara responded. She knew that she no longer fit in with many of her friends.

"Bye," Susanna replied, and hung up the phone.

Kara was saddened, though not surprised, by her friend's response. Though Susanna claimed to be a Christian, this was probably too much for her to swallow. Kara knew that she really was changed. It was difficult to focus on the things of this world any longer. They were all meaningless to her. Her love for Jesus overshadowed her, leaving the world around her hollow and void compared to his presence. She missed Him terribly.

The party was a lot of fun. Grandma came, and Dad, Mama, and Jeremy were there. They had chocolate cake with vanilla icing and chocolate ice cream. They had soda, though Kara drank milk, as the soda burned her throat. The five of them laughed and played silly games, mostly guessing games. Kara's room was filled with balloons, and confetti was everywhere. Jeremy helped her open the gifts. Grandma gave her rose perfume, Dad gave her a cross necklace, Mama gave her the tape player/recorder, and Jeremy gave her some worship tapes, besides some empty tapes in case she wanted to record anything. Secretly, Jeremy wanted to record the things she shared with him about Jesus. Guiding her hand, Jeremy showed her how to work the player, and though her efforts were clumsy, she succeeded. Smiles and peace permeated the room.

When it was time for Grandma to leave, David and Savannah prepared to take her home. "Why don't you go with them, Jeremy," Kara suggested. "I'd like to be alone." Reluctantly, her brother obeyed, knowing it was useless to argue. Kara gave each a hug and a kiss, and they were off.

Her recorder beside her bed, Kara decided to try a worship tape. She slipped one into the player and pushed the buttons, but she heard nothing. Before she could reach to check for the problem, she heard a loud noise at the front door. It sounded as if someone had knocked the door in. She fought the desire to be afraid. Whatever came, her King was with her. Someone was in the house. It sounded as if they were going room to room, throwing open the doors.

As Kara's door flung open, a man stood before her. He looked like an older version of Daniel, with his short, dark hair and flashing brown eyes. He was heavier, bearing a beer belly on his six foot two frame. He looked angry, and Kara knew instinctively who he was. Though she had never met him, Daniel told her about his father, who at the time was in prison. The resemblance was incredible.

"What did you do to my boy?" he screamed. Kara had no idea what to say. He hurled obscenities at her, and screamed again, "What did you do to Daniel? Why are you alive and he is dead?" Still Kara could not reply. The man shut the door behind him, presumably to limit the noise from carrying, and stormed over to Kara's bed. She knew she could not escape the man, so she remained still.

"I'm sorry he died," she whispered.

"I bet you are! You will be by the time I am done with you!" The man began tearing Kara's clothes from her, and she started to cry, sure he was about to rape her. But when he looked at her scarred frame, he screamed again, "I don't have sex with freaks! But you are going to pay! You will wish you had died with the rest of them before I am done, and rape would feel better than what I will do to you now!" Those lashes had spared her one torment, at least, disallowing the loss of what she considered to be her most precious personal worldly possession. But the man pulled off his belt and started beating the child, as she lay helpless and naked before him. He unleashed a fury upon her, not caring where the belt landed. He struck her repeatedly, hitting her face, her chest, her stomach, and every other part of her he could. As the belt buckle hit her indiscriminately in the eye, she though about what her Lord had taught her, that the punishments of men were both cruel and ineffective. They were not as the correction of her Lord, for in those lashes was found mercy, and He had taken them with her. Not satisfied with his efforts, the man turned her body about, making sure he struck her in every fashion he found possible. The buckle landed and caught on the scars, tearing at her flesh. His belt seemed to land everywhere, ripping at her entire form, her body fully exposed to his rage. His fury went on a long while, but she did not cry out. Pain was no stranger to her. As she did not respond, he became angrier and angrier, thrashing with all his might. "What did you do?" he screamed. "I know you did something! They said all five of those kids were screaming for God's forgiveness, and all you did was go to sleep! And you are the only one who woke up!" He continued to beat her in a frenzy and became even more furious when he saw a faint smile cross her face. This crazed man had unknowingly delivered her birthday present! She now knew that the other children had cried out for God. Though it had been necessary for her to face her sin without this comfort, God was reassuring her now. Even in this most horrific moment, there was a bit of comfort for her. The man was so infuriated that he began to beat her with other objects lying about the room. He hurled books at her, and even threw a lamp, trying anything to extinguish the smile she wore. He pulled down a certain rod and hit her with it repeatedly, even causing cuts form the end of the tool, until he seemed to have expended all his energy. He punched her repeatedly with his fists and kicked her with his boots. No amount of brutality seemed to satisfy the hate within this man. Finally pulling out a knife, Daniel's father grabbed her by the hair, pulled her head back, and he held the razor sharp blade to her throat. "What do you think now, missy?" he growled. "Still think you got by with something? You are about to die!"

"I forgive you," she whispered. "Jesus loves you! Lord, please forgive him! He really doesn't understand!" Before the words lodged into the heart of the man, his knife had made its way through her throat, and she was gone. As the words landed, however, the man dropped her limp body and ran screaming into the night.

....

As David, Savannah, and Jeremy arrived home, they were accosted by a terrible sight. The front door was broken in, with bloody hand prints on the frame. Fear gripped at their hearts. Blood was tracked from the house into the street. Jeremy ran ahead, ignoring everyone's caution. He had to know what had become of his sister. Rushing to her room, he ran hysterically back to the couple, crying out that she was gone. Not able to ascertain exactly what had taken place, David raced into the room, his heart in his throat. Jeremy held Savannah back. As David looked upon the child, he remembered the haunting words, "will you forgive him?" He called the police, but Savannah refused to be held any longer and entered the room. All were weeping at the torn frame. Who would have done this? Jeremy's eyes wandered throughout the room, landing on the balloons and birthday gifts. He saw the perfume from Grandma, and Kara still wore the necklace her Daddy had given her.

Then he saw the tape player. It seemed to be running, so he decided to turn it off. As he reached over, however, he noted something of interest. In her clumsiness, Kara had placed an empty tape in the machine and hit record! Though he knew he would likely be chided by the police, they were not there yet, and he had to know. Rewinding the tape, he played it back, revealing the entire story. It took the police longer than usual to arrive, and though it was painful to hear, they played the tape. As the police entered, it was as if a holy hush stopped them in their tracks, and they let it play on. Savannah marveled in her heart that Kara did not cry out, and as Kara forgave the man, all three remembered the words of their Lord from the night before. Kara forgave the man, and no matter how painful it was, they knew they could do no less. Her words lodged into the hearts of the police as well. None would be untouched by what had transpired here.

The three left, escorted from the premises by the police, their hearts sick with disgust and sorrow. Looking back towards the house, Jeremy noticed the bloody hand prints on both sides of the door. Though he knew that there was no redemption in any other than the blood of Jesus, it still reminded him of the Passover lamb and the feast, when the angel of death passed over the children of Israel. It was a symbol to him of his Lord's love for his family. There would be a painful road ahead, but Kara had forged the way. They spent a sleepless night together at Grandma's, talking over many things. Jeremy told the couple about Kara's requests, and that she had been talking about dying for some time. They all agreed that they would honor her as she had desired and that Jeremy would speak at the funeral. Together they took their comfort in the Lord.

....

Daniel's father was apprehended that same night, and the evidence was clear against him. He was practically incoherent anyway, as he could not shake the words of this little girl. How could she forgive him as she was about to die? Throughout his torments, she had never cried out against him. He had hurt other people before, but none had responded this way. He was so distressed he could not think. As morning approached, the guards greeted him with a letter. As he read it, his hands began to shake. Apparently Kara's family had tried to visit him and had been turned away. They had left a note. It merely read: "We forgive you. What you have taken from us is more precious than you can know, or you could not have done this, but God loves you. We forgive you because He has asked it of us. Kara forgave you as she was dying, and we can do no less. We hope you will accept God's forgiveness for you." All three had signed the note. The man began to weep and groan uncontrollably, and he begged to see a chaplain. That night he accepted Jesus as his Lord, and though he knew he had severe consequences to face, he decided that he would no longer try to beat the rap as he had so often done. He knew that whatever judgment was passed on him was infinitely less than he deserved. For the first time in his life, he threw himself on the mercy of the Lord. Though he would likely receive the death penalty for what he had done, he was at peace.

Asking for writing supplies, the man penned a reply. He apologized to the family for the anguish he had caused and thanked them for their note. He did not even care if the note was used against him in a court of law, as he was prepared to confess all that he had done. He knew his confession would clear up many other crimes as well.

It was a mere matter of formality to process the evidence against Kara's killer, and her body was soon available to be put to rest. Her three family members marveled at how effectively the morticians covered her scarring. Jeremy prepared for the task at hand. As Kara had predicted, he knew what the poem she had given him was for. It was to be engraved on her headstone.

Chapter 11

Kara saw the arms of her Savior reaching out to her, as He pulled her from this place. She sighed a deep sigh of the deepest relief. This darkness was finally done. Though she knew that Jesus' blood had been shed long ago and that His was the only redemptive sacrifice, she felt that symbolically the blood had been poured from the bucket, and the Fire of the Holy Spirit had been unleashed as she forgave the man.

As her King pulled her from this chasm, she thought she passed Stephan on the way. She saw the martyrs of old, and each saluted her. The words of Hebrews 12:1-2 echoed within her, "Therefore we also, since we are surrounded by so great a cloud of witnesses, let us lay aside every weight, and the sin which so easily ensnares us, and let us run with endurance the race that is set before us, looking unto Jesus, the author and finisher of our faith, who for the joy that was set before Him endured the cross, despising the shame, and has sat down at the right hand of the throne of God." (NKJV) He took her and bathed her again, in His Holy Blood, in His Word, and in His Fire. She wept continually, tears of joy and relief at escaping that horrible, dirty place, and she was in His arms again. Calling her by her new name, He held her firmly. "Well done!" He proclaimed. "Well done!" Celestial beings attended her, as she donned a new body and royal robes. Not a single scar remained, only endless jewels with fragrances that sent ecstasy throughout her frame. The child was so enthralled by the majesty of this place that she nearly forgot the darkness from which she had just come.

Taking her hand, the King held her close, pulling her against His breast. "I have missed you, little one," His gentle Voice fluttered through her. "Happy birthday. It is so very good to have you home." Kara was content to rest upon His chest, weary from that long, dark eternal night. She was finally with Him again. "You will never again be so far from My presence," His comforting words echoed through her being. "The purging is complete. After you rest for a bit, I want to show you something." She cried tears of joy, releasing all the pain within her, and He wiped her tears away. His Voice rippled through her being once again, exciting every segment of her soul. As she clung to Him, every ounce of her person cried out never to be separated from Him again.

"Kara," He began, "do you remember that unspoken thought? You once wanted to see your own funeral, didn't you?" She smiled sheepishly. "You wanted to pretend that it was so you could see if anyone got saved, but at the time, you had another reason."

"I wanted to hear what they would say about me," she replied.

"Would the reason be the same now?"

"No, Lord. That was pride. Now I really would like to see if anyone got saved."

Her Savior smiled. "Let's watch!" He said, somewhat in a hushed Voice as if in fun. "This should be interesting. Let Us comfort them in their grief." The two stood above the earth, looking on as the doors of a church opened, and the funeral began.

....

Savannah walked by the casket of her child. Her grief was overpowering. How could she lose her daughter for the second time? This last year had truly been an emotional roller coaster, leaving her sick at heart beyond measure. Kara's nine months in a coma had brought the delivery of a beautiful young woman Savannah barely knew, only for her to be snatched away again. Looking upon her small form, Kara seemed radiant in her light green dress. The scars were barely visible, and Savannah supposed the makeup job was exceptionally well done. She was startled, however, to look at Kara's left hand. Someone had placed the most elegant pale green jewel in a ring on her ring finger. It was as nothing she had ever seen before. Touching it, she noticed that it did not budge, and she wondered at the sight. It covered the scar from when her finger was severed in the accident. Grilling David and Jeremy, she found that no one knew from where the ring had come. Even the mortician claimed to have no knowledge of its source. Observing this, Kara smiled at her King.

Jeremy walked to the front, wearing a dark blue suit. Kara was pleased to note that they were allowing him to do the entire ceremony. The room was packed with people, while many more stood outside. Even hospital workers were there. Her therapist came, police officers came, and Jackie and Susanna attended as well. There were amplifiers positioned so that the people outside could also hear the service. David was seated with Savannah at the front, as he donned his black suit and Savannah wore a long black dress. Jeremy began his speech with eloquence, though his intense emotions had been difficult to restrain.

"Today we honor a very special young woman," he began brokenly. "She was my sister, but more than that, she was my friend." Catching his breath that was filled with great passion, he went on. "The things I have to say today are the things she taught me, and many she asked that I share with you some day. I never dreamed it would be so soon. You see, she knew she would soon be with her King, though undoubtedly she did not know how it would take place. Yet if she had known, she undoubtedly would have embraced it all the same. She would have accepted any route that brought her to Him. Kara had a love affair with Jesus that transformed her life. She understood that Jesus died to save us from sin. In her own words, she explained her concept of God quite eloquently. She spoke these things when the press insisted on an answer to sum up what she felt was important: 'Jesus loves us all incredibly. He loves us with a passion. But He equally detests sin. He will do anything to get us to give it up. We never really get by with sin. He died so we wouldn't have to suffer the consequences of what we have done, but if we refuse what He offers, the consequences are worse than we can ever imagine. Even after He saves us, we have to let Him heal us from sin. It is a terrible disease.

But if we obey, being with Him is more wonderful than anything, and any amount of suffering is worth it, just to be with Him.' Kara believed in a God who loves us. But she never shirked her responsibility before Him for her sin. She taught that we are all fatally flawed by its nature in us and that we have to face it and denounce its place in our lives. She was willing to suffer, to accept His chastening, in order to be truly free from sin."

"Today we live in a world that balks against God's judgment, though He has suffered greatly to rescue us all. We presume to think that God should tolerate our sin rather than to remove it from us. We mock our Maker, declaring Him unjust when He teaches us through suffering. We truly do not grasp the very holiness of God. He is seeking to change our very hearts, where the roots of evil dwell; and cleaning up our actions is not enough for Him. As Kara taught us, He truly finds sin as utterly despicable."

"Many have memorized John 3:16, but we need to read further. Today I read to you John 3:16-21: 'For God so loved the world that He gave His only begotten Son, that whoever believes in Him should not perish but have everlasting life. For God did not send His Son into the world to condemn the world, but that the world through Him might be saved. He who believes in Him is not condemned; but he who does not believe is condemned already, because he has not believed in the name of the only begotten Son of God. **And this is the condemnation, that the light has come into the world, and men loved darkness rather than light, because their deeds were evil.** For everyone practicing evil hates the light and does not come to the light, lest his deeds should be exposed. But he who does the truth comes to the light, that his deeds may be clearly seen, that they have been done in God.' (NKJV)" Kara served a God who requires honesty before Him. She knew a Savior who demands that men allow their deeds to be brought into the light. Yet we have sat idly by, refusing to own up to our own shortcomings, that we might be healed. We have preferred to cling to our sins rather than to renounce them. The wonderful Lord that Kara fell in love with, that she cried out to see, is interested in our complete redemption, not just in getting us to Heaven. Though we get there, we will not escape facing Him for unrepentant sin."

"Kara was enraptured by her love of this King, not considering for a moment that His tactics were too harsh, as she understood what we do not. She understood, as I quoted, that He 'loves us incredibly....But He equally detests sin.' She was willing to rejoice in her suffering rather than to complain that His dealings were cruel, for she saw those dealings as His kindness that brings us to repentance. She took the words of Hebrews quite literally. Hebrews 12:5-9 states it clearly: 'And you have forgotten the exhortation which speaks to you as to sons: "My son, do not despise the chastening of the LORD, Nor be discouraged when you are rebuked by Him; For whom the LORD loves He chastens, And scourges every son whom He receives." If you endure chastening, God deals with you as with sons; for what son is there whom a father does not chasten? But if you are without chastening, of which all have become partakers, then you are illegitimate and not sons.

Furthermore, we have had human fathers who corrected us, and we paid them respect. Shall we not much more readily be in subjection to the Father of spirits and live?' (NKJV) We whine and complain against a God Who has suffered for us and Who, according to Kara, still suffers with us. She once told me that 'the cross is merely a summation of all the horror of the ages', a central point of focus for all the sufferings of the Savior. She did not view Jesus as a tyrant who watched while we suffered. Rather, she understood the words of Hebrews 5:8-9, 'though He was a Son, yet He learned obedience by the things which He suffered. And having been perfected, He became the author of eternal salvation to all who obey Him,' (NKJV). She understood that even Jesus, especially Jesus, suffered, and according to scripture, learned through that suffering."

"I ask today that you consider the words of Hebrews 2:2-3, 'For if the word spoken through angels proved steadfast, and every transgression and disobedience received a just reward, how shall we escape if we neglect so great a salvation, which at the first began to be spoken by the Lord, and was confirmed to us by those who heard Him,' (NKJV). I ask today that you contemplate the scripture, that you consider Kara's God, as revealed in Romans 11:22, 'Therefore consider the goodness and severity of God: on those who fell, severity; but toward you, goodness, if you continue in His goodness. Otherwise you also will be cut off.' (NKJV). We saw her life, and it was a testimony of His greatness. Today she is the epitome of the verse in 1 Peter, chapter four, verse one: 'Therefore, since Christ suffered for us in the flesh, arm yourselves also with the same mind, for he who has suffered in the flesh has ceased from sin,' (NLJV). "

"I ask today that you heed the scriptures, as noted again in Hebrews 3:7-13, 'Therefore, as the Holy Spirit says: "Today, if you will hear His voice, Do not harden your hearts as in the rebellion, In the day of trial in the wilderness, Where your fathers tested Me, tried Me, And saw My works forty years. Therefore I was angry with that generation, And said, 'They always go astray in their heart, And they have not known My ways.' So I swore in My wrath, 'They shall not enter My rest.' Beware, brethren, lest there be in any of you an evil heart of unbelief in departing from the living God; but exhort one another daily, while it is called "Today," lest any of you be hardened through the deceitfulness of sin.' (NKJV) Ladies and gentlemen, I ask that you take seriously the following passage, as God is speaking clearly to us now. 2 Corinthians 6:2, 'For He says: "In an acceptable time I have heard you, And in the day of salvation I have helped you." Behold, now is the accepted time; behold, now is the day of salvation.' (NKJV)."

"If you, like myself, have been pricked to the core, than it is required that you respond. Kara once told me that when you are brought into God's presence, whatever you decide at that moment becomes sealed. You can be made solid in your repentance, or you can greatly deepen your sin. Our answer is again in Romans, chapter 10, verses eight through eleven: 'But what does it say? "The word is near you, in your mouth and in your heart" (that is, the word of faith which we preach): that if you confess with your mouth the Lord

Jesus and believe in your heart that God has raised Him from the dead, you will be saved. For with the heart one believes unto righteousness, and with the mouth confession is made unto salvation. For the Scripture says, "Whoever believes on Him will not be put to shame." ' (NKJV) If you truly want to know Him, to meet Kara's God, boldly join me in this, for I will not, as Paul states in Romans, be 'ashamed of the gospel'. I read you his words in chapter one, verse sixteen, 'For I am not ashamed of the gospel of Christ, for it is the power of God to salvation for everyone who believes, for the Jew first and also for the Greek.' (NKJV) If you will join me in confessing with your mouth, please pray aloud with me. Father, I know I have sinned. You paid a great price for my sin through Jesus on the cross, and You raised Him from the dead. I accept that sacrifice and I ask for Your forgiveness. I confess that I have sinned, and I accept that You will cleanse me. Though I may suffer, I will praise You and know that You are just. Please help me to always walk in this, and when I stumble, pick me up. I accept Jesus as my Lord and my Savior. Amen."

Nearly everyone in the place was weeping deeply, some quite audibly. They all prayed with him, all including Jackie, the police, and the therapist. Kara watched as an elderly gentleman approached Jeremy. "Son," he said. "I'd like to be your mentor to help you get ordained as a minister." He paused. "It won't cost you anything." Jeremy nodded, giving the man his contact information. Then he looked again into the coffin at the body of his sister and gasped. Pulling David and Savannah over, he pointed to her left hand. Next to the green jeweled ring rested the most beautiful golden wedding band. Kara smiled at her Savior, tears of joy filling her eyes. Holding a seed in her hands, she turned to her Lord for permission, and He nodded in agreement. She dropped it on Jeremy, whispering, "Tonight I will see you in your dreams." Jeremy would dream of brighter days, playing with Kara as though they were little children again. He would hear her laugh and see her run, unscarred by this world of sin. He would hear her whisper, "Buy Mama a dress. Tell her she does not look good in black. Tell her We will be waiting, Jesus and me, for when she comes to us. But she needs to wait a while. Tell her not to be too sad. She has you now. And Jeremy, you can call her Mama if you like. Tell Daddy We love him too. We love you, Jeremy. You were such a blessing to me. Tell everyone to be wise and use their time on Earth to deal with their sin. And please forgive me, but I won't be watching. I will be completely enthralled with Him."

She blew one last kiss to Daddy, one to Mama, and two to Jeremy. Elisha received his double portion, she thought with a smile. They all seemed to sense her kisses landing, though they surely did not know what it meant. She was giving each a bit of herself, each a memory of her love for Jesus. She simply blew them each a kiss and turned away to go with her Maker, never to look back again. Jeremy wrote a poem for her, which he placed in her casket.

The journey was long;

she opened her eyes

that she might ponder

and be wise

as to what her life

was built upon....

A parade of figures

was marching by,

each with a song,

a word,

a cry.

Children sang merrily,

dancing free,

with uplifted voices

proclaiming to her,

"Your life

meant something

to me!"

The parade continued
as those with whom
she had shared
her toil
steadily crossed
the trodden soil...

She heard their voices
lifted high
in choruses free...
"Your life
meant something
to me!"

Person by person,
crowds and crowds,
they came from
the seas,
the lands,
the clouds...

Each with a story
to relate
of how her life
had changed
his fate...

Each reported faithfully,
"Your life meant something
to me!"

Quietly she regained
her voice,
to ask a question
of the Rock
of her choice.

She softly pleaded
to comprehend
why she was
not yet satisfied.

"Though truly You
have chosen me,
I am not ungrateful
this sight to see....
but is there not
something more
than these?"

He kindly reached
with nail-scarred hands,
touched her face
that she might know
that He could
understand...

Then He spoke
the words that
brought her peace....

"As you did it
for the least of these,
it was for Me
that you would please."

"You wiped my tears,
you washed my face,
with great grace
you ran the race."

"Your life meant
EVERYTHING to Me!
It was built
upon Jesus the Rock."

"You have done
faithfully.
Well done!
Sit here with Me!"

Chapter 12

Jesus ushered Kara to a great banquet. A large table was filled with foods of every sort, most of which Kara had never seen or even imagined. "Kara, you can eat now, and your throat will not hurt any more. Come, I want you to meet My Father. We have been waiting for this for so long! You are My guest of honor today!"

Seated at the head of the table, His glory met her before she could rest Her eyes upon Him. So majestic was His form and bright His radiance that none could begin to describe Him. She fell on her face before Him, but with a single finger, He lifted her to Himself, displaying the most brilliant smile. "Welcome home, child! Well done! You may now enter the joy of your King!" Rapture encompassed her as she gloried in His presence. She was seated beside Jesus, and a multitude of the martyrs of old, each now intricately enmeshed into His presence and His being, joined in the celebration. They sang joyous songs of the redeemed, lifting their voices as one to their King. They knew that her voice could now join with theirs in their glorious song. When all were seated, the feast began. Day upon eternal day, they laughed and ate, enjoying the holiness of the place. There was only light, for darkness had been banished, and death was swallowed up. No time moved them to leave that glorious place. The magnificence of the dining hall was beyond description as the least thing of value was greater than anything she had seen before. Yet even this was nothing compared to Him. She no longer knew pain, for her suffering was complete. She need not visit it again.

As if this ecstasy were not enough, her Lord took her by the hand and raised her from her seat at the table. He seemed overjoyed and ecstatic beyond measure as He conversed with her. "Love," He whispered, and called her by her most holy name, the one known to the two of them alone, "let Us begin the wedding!" The awe so captured her that she could only look into His face, making no motion to move. Celestial beings stood with her, trading her royal robes for the most superb wedding gown ever formed. It was whiter than the most brilliant light, lined with a treasure much like gold, yet finer. They poured their perfumes upon her, adorning every part of her person with the finest jewels. With this, she was so enthralled with her Lord that she could not even look at what had been placed upon her. The thrill of His presence resounded through every cell of her being, the very fiber of her form quivering in expectation. She could not remove her eyes from His glory. Every part of her cried out to be one with Him, that she be so enveloped that she cease her separate existence completely. They walked along a golden path where flower pedals covered their way. Kara could only look at Him, absorbing His magnificence. All else was insignificant. This was the summation of her entire desire, all enveloped in Him. She was sure she would die an eternal death if they were ever apart, for now He encompassed her every thread, and she knew no fear of separation. She knew that she was His eternally and that none could remove her from His hand.

Voices of the most radiant praises and music of pure ecstasy encompassed them. Yet she could only see Him, her very self determined to only hear His Voice. All creation marveled at the wonder before them as they looked upon her face, His face, as they merged into all the excellence of the ages. The pair stood before the Father, with His white flowing hair and radiance surpassing description. They stood upon what appeared as a sea of glass, shining in brilliance. His Majesty and Light encompassed them, as they spoke their vows one to another, promising without reservation that they would never part. The eyes of her King were like a fire that consumed her, as she was pulled every moment more deeply into their grasp. His depth was infinite, and she wanted nothing more than to be drawn further and further into Him. Kara barely knew when the ceremony was complete, as He placed His eternal ring upon her hand. Celestial beings were prostrate before Him. The Father planted His kiss upon her cheek, and the two walked further on.

Looking deeply into those magnificent Eyes, Kara asked her Lord one more question. "Lord, how is it that You can have such an amazing relationship with each one of Your children, as if each was the most important to you?"

"Each of you is an integral part of My Bride. I am infinitely so huge compared to you that as you become consumed in My presence, you are as a single cell that is lodged in its own particular residence in Me. Each part of the Body has its own place, a particular portion in Me that is shared by no one else. That dwelling is designed especially for you. No one else can fill this space, for you were the one created for it. Each of you has a name known to none but to the individual and to Me. Each has an intimacy very private between us, a song and a voice known only to the two of Us. Though you are all a part of the whole, there is no time to place a restraint upon us in eternity, which means you can each perceive your union with Me as occurring separately without compromising the whole. Yet in this most holy bliss, there is a waiting until all is fulfilled, that the Body may be one, whole and complete in Me. It is a mystery to be sure, as your mind can not encompass it." Speaking her most holy name, He continued, "It's time to go in, to finalize the work that was begun." His Voice reverberated through all that she was. His brilliant smile and fiery eyes enveloped her, and she was memorizing Him feature by feature, an endless task that she desired to prolong forever. "I have prepared a place for you as I have promised. The inner chamber of your heart has been made complete," His mighty Voice proclaimed. As they entered that most holy place of all, she barely saw the awe inspiring inscriptions He had written there, so mesmerized was she with her King. No other being was granted viewing of those fabulous inscriptions, so carefully engraved there. The large majestic doors were closed behind them, covered in His blood, as He carried her in. All eternity turned its head to look away, unable to partake in this particular holiness. This moment was for these two alone.

"You are all fair, my love, And there is no spot in you." Song of Songs 4:7 (NKJV)

"You have ravished my heart, My sister, my spouse; You have ravished my heart With one look of your eyes, With one link of your necklace. How fair is your love, My sister, my spouse! How much better than wine is your love, And the scent of your perfumes Than all spices!" Song of Songs 4:9-10 (NKJV)